D1592479

CAPE EDITIONS 39

General Editor: NATHANIEL TARN

# Genesis as
## Myth

AND OTHER ESSAYS

# Edmund
## Leach

JONATHAN CAPE
THIRTY BEDFORD SQUARE
LONDON

This collection first published 1969
by Jonathan Cape Ltd, 30 Bedford Square,
London, WC1
© 1969 by Edmund Leach
'Genesis as Myth' first appeared in *Discovery*
(now incorporated in *Science Journal*), vol. XXIII,
May 1962
'The Legitimacy of Solomon' first appeared in *European
Journal of Sociology*, vol. VII, 1966, 58–101
'Virgin Birth' first appeared in *Proceedings of the
Royal Anthropological Institute of Great Britain and
Ireland*, 1966

SBN Paperback edition 224 61782 6
      Hardback edition 224 61780 X

Printed and bound in Great Britain
by Richard Clay (The Chaucer Press), Ltd
Bungay, Suffolk

# Contents

GENESIS AS MYTH 7

THE LEGITIMACY OF SOLOMON 25

VIRGIN BIRTH 85

NOTES 113

SELECTED BIBLIOGRAPHY 123

A NOTE ON THE AUTHOR 124

# GENESIS AS MYTH*

A distinguished German theologian has defined myth
as 'the expression of unobservable realities in terms
of observable phenomena.'[1] All stories which occur in
the Bible are myths for the devout Christian, whether
they correspond to historical fact or not. All human
societies have myths in this sense, and normally the
myths to which the greatest importance is attached
are those which are the least probable. The non-
rationality of myth is its very essence, for religion
requires a demonstration of faith by the suspension of
critical doubt.

But if myths do not mean what they appear to
mean, how do they come to mean anything at all?
What is the nature of the esoteric mode of communication by which myth is felt to give 'expression
to unobservable realities'?

This is an old problem which has lately taken on a
new shape because, if myth be a mode of communication, then a part of the theory which is embodied in
digital computer systems ought to be relevant. The
merit of this approach is that it draws special attention to precisely those features of myth which have
formerly been regarded as accidental defects. It is
common to all mythological systems that all important stories recur in several different versions. Man
is created in Genesis (i. 27) and then he is created all
over again (ii. 7). And, as if two first men were not

*References such as (iv. 3) refer to the third verse of the
fourth chapter of the book of Genesis (English Authorized
Version) unless otherwise stated.

7

enough, we also have Noah in chapter viii. Likewise in the New Testament, why must there be four gospels each telling the 'same' story yet sometimes flatly contradictory on details of fact? Another notice-able characteristic of mythical stories is their markedly binary aspect; myth is constantly setting up opposing categories: 'In the beginning God created the heaven and the earth'; 'They crucified Him and two others with him, on either side one, and Jesus in the midst'; 'I am the Alpha and the Omega, the be-ginning and the end, saith the Lord.' So always it is in myth – God against the world and the world itself for ever dividing into opposites on either side: male and female, living and dead, good and evil, first and last ...

Now, in the language of communication engineers, the first of these common characteristics of myth is called *redundancy*, while the second is strongly reminiscent of the unit of information – the *bit*. 'In-formation' in this technical sense is a measure of the freedom of choice in selecting a message. If there are only two messages and it is arbitrary which you choose then 'information is unity', that is = 1 bit.*[2]

Communication engineers employ these concepts for the analysis of problems which arise when a par-ticular individual (the sender) wishes to transmit a coded message correctly to another individual (the receiver) against a background of interference (noise). 'Information' refers on the one hand to the degrees of choice open to the sender in encoding his transmission, and on the other to the degrees of choice open to the receiver in interpreting what he receives (which will include noise in addition to the original transmitted signal). In this situation a high level of redundancy makes it easy to correct errors introduced by noise.

* Bit stands for 'binary digit'.

Now in the mind of the believer, myth does indeed convey messages which are the Word of God. To such a man the redundancy of myth is a very reassuring fact. Any particular myth in isolation is like a coded message badly snarled up with noisy interference. Even the most confident devotee might feel a little uncertain as to what precisely is being said. But, as a result of redundancy, the believer can feel that, even when the details vary, each alternative version of a myth confirms his understanding and reinforces the essential meaning of all the others.

The anthropologist's viewpoint is different. He rejects the idea of a supernatural sender. He observes only a variety of possible receivers. Here redundancy increases information – that is the uncertainty of the possible means of decoding the message. This explains what is surely the most striking of all religious phenomena – the passionate adherence to sectarian belief. The whole of Christendom shares a single corpus of mythology so it is surely very remarkable that the members of each particular Christian sect are able to convince themselves that they alone possess the secret of revealed truth. The abstract propositions of communication theory help us to understand this paradox.

But if the true believer can interpret his own mythology in almost any way he chooses, what principle governs the formation of the original myth? Is it random chance that a myth assumes one pattern rather than another? The binary structure of myth suggests otherwise.

Binary oppositions are intrinsic to the process of human thought. Any description of the world must discriminate categories in the form '*p* is what not-*p* is not'. An object is alive or not alive and one could not formulate the concept 'alive' except as the converse of its partner 'dead'. So also human beings are male or not male, and persons of the opposite sex are either available as sexual partners or not available. Universally these are the most fundamentally important oppositions in all human experience.

Religion everywhere is preoccupied with the first, the antinomy of life and death. Religion seeks to deny the binary link between the two words; it does this by creating the mystical idea of 'another world', a land of the dead where life is perpetual. The attributes of this other world are necessarily those which are not of this world; imperfection here is balanced by perfection there. But this logical ordering of ideas has a disconcerting consequence – God comes to belong to the other world. The central 'problem' of religion is then to re-establish some kind of bridge between Man and God.

This pattern is built into the structure of every mythical system; the myth first discriminates between gods and men and then becomes preoccupied with the relations and intermediaries which link men and gods together. This much is already implicit in our initial definition.

So too with sex relations. Every human society has rules of incest and exogamy. Though the rules vary they always have the implication that for any particular male individual all women are divided by at least one binary distinction, there are women of *our kind* with whom sex relations would be incestuous and there are women of the *other kind* with whom sex relations are allowed. But here again we are immediately led into paradox. How was it in the beginning? If our first parents were persons of two kinds, what was that other kind? But if they were both of our kind, then their relations must have been incestuous and we are all born in sin. The myths of the world offer many different solutions to this childish intellectual puzzle, but the prominence which it receives shows that it entails the most profound moral issues. The crux is as before. If the logic of our thought leads us to distinguish *we* from *they*, how can we bridge the gap and establish social and sexual relations with 'the others' without throwing our categories into confusion?

So, despite all variations of theology, this aspect of myth is a constant. In every myth system we will find a persistent sequence of binary discriminations as between human/superhuman, mortal/immortal, male/female, legitimate/illegitimate, good/bad ... followed by a 'mediation' of the paired categories thus distinguished.

'Mediation' (in this sense) is always achieved by introducing a third category which is 'abnormal' or 'anomalous' in terms of ordinary 'rational' categories. Thus myths are full of fabulous monsters, incarnate gods, virgin mothers. This middle ground is abnormal, non-natural, holy. It is typically the focus of all taboo and ritual observance.

This approach to myth analysis derives originally from the techniques of structural linguistics associated with the name of Roman Jakobson[3] but is more immediately due to Claude Lévi-Strauss, one of whose examples may serve to illustrate the general principle.

Certain Pueblo Indian myths focus on the opposition between life and death. In these myths we find a threefold category distinction: agriculture (means to life), war (means to death), and hunting (a mediating category since it is means to life for men but means to death for animals). Other myths of the same cluster deploy a different triad: grass-eating animals (which live without killing), predators (which live by killing), and carrion-eating creatures (mediators, since they eat meat but do not kill in order to eat). In accumulation this total set of associated symbols serves to imply that life and death are *not* just the back and the front of the same penny, that death is *not* the necessary consequence of life.[4]

My Fig. 1 has been designed to display an analogous structure for the case of the first four chapters of Genesis. The three horizontal bands of the diagram correspond to (i) the story of the seven-day creation, (ii) the story of the Garden of Eden, and (iii) the story of Cain and Abel. The diagram can also be read vertically: column 1 in band (ii) corresponds to column 1 in band (i) and so on. The detailed analysis is as follows:—

UPPER BAND

*First Day.* (i. 1–5; not on diagram). Heaven distinguished from Earth; Light from Darkness; Day from Night; Evening from Morning.

*Second Day.* (i. 6–8; col. 1 of diagram). (Fertile) water (rain) above; (infertile) water (sea) below. Mediated by firmament (sky).

*Third Day.* (i. 9–10; col. 2 and i. 11–12; col. 3). Sea opposed to dry land. Mediated by 'grass, herb-yielding seed (cereals), fruit trees'. These grow on dry land but need water. They are classed as things 'whose seed is in itself' and thereby contrasted with bisexual animals, birds, etc.

The creation of the world as a static (that is, dead) entity is now complete and this whole phase of the creation is opposed to the creation of moving (that is, living) things.

*Fourth Day.* (i. 13–18; col. 4). Mobile sun and moon are placed in the fixed firmament of col. 1. Light and darkness become alternations (life and death become alternates).

*Fifth Day.* (i. 20–3; col. 5). Fish and birds are living things corresponding to the sea/land opposition of col. 2 but they also mediate the col. 1 oppositions between sky and earth and between salt water and fresh water.

*Sixth Day.* (i. 24–5; col. 6). Cattle (domestic animals), beasts (wild animals), creeping things. These correspond to the static triad of col. 3. But only the grass is allocated to the animals. Everything else, including the meat of the animals, is for Man's use (i. 29–30). Later at Leviticus xi creatures which do not fit this exact ordering of the world – for instance water creatures with no fins, animals and birds which eat meat or fish, etc. – are classed as 'abominations' Creeping Things are anomalous with respect to the major categories, Fowl, Fish, Cattle, Beast, and are thus abominations *ab initio* (Leviticus xi. 41–2). This classification in turn leads to an anomalous contradiction. In order to allow the Israelites to eat locusts the author of Leviticus xi had to introduce a special qualification to the prohibition against eating creeping things: 'Yet these ye *may* eat: of every flying creeping thing that goeth on all four which have legs above their feet, to leap withal upon the earth' (v. 21). The procedures of binary discrimination could scarcely be carried further!

(i. 26–7; col. 7). Man and Woman are created simultaneously.

The whole system of living creatures is instructed to 'be fruitful and multiply', but the problems of Life versus Death, and Incest versus Procreation are not faced at all.

CENTRE BAND

The Garden of Eden story which now follows tackles from the start these very problems which have been

evaded in the first version. We start again with the
opposition Heaven versus Earth, but this is mediated
by a fertilizing mist drawn from the dry infertile
earth (ii. 4–6). This theme, which blurs the distinction
life/death, is repeated. Living Adam is formed from
the dead dust of the ground (ii. 7); so are the animals
(ii. 19); the garden is fertilized by a river which 'went
out of Eden' (ii. 10); finally fertile Eve is formed from
a rib of infertile Adam (ii. 22–3).

The opposition Heaven/Earth is followed by further
oppositions – Man/Garden (ii. 15); Tree of Life/Tree of
Death (ii. 9, 17); the latter is called the tree of the
'knowledge of good and evil' which means the knowledge of sexual difference.

Recurrent also is the theme that unity in the other
world (Eden, Paradise) becomes duality in this world.
Outside Eden the river splits into four and divides the
world into separate lands (ii. 10–14). In Eden, Adam
can exist by himself, Life can exist by itself; in this
world, there are men and women, life and death. This
repeats the contrast between monosexual plants and
bisexual animals which is stressed in the first story.

The other living creatures are now created specifically because of the loneliness of Man in Eden (ii. 18).
The categories are Cattle, Birds, Beasts. None of these
are adequate as a helpmeet for Man. So finally Eve is
drawn from Adam's rib ... 'they are of one flesh'
(ii. 18–24).

Comparison of Band 1 and Band 2 at this stage
shows that Eve in the second story replaces the 'Creeping Things' of the first story. Just as Creeping Things
were anomalous with respect to Fish, Fowl, Cattle and
Beast so Eve is anomalous to the opposition Man
versus Animal. And, as a final mediation (chapter iii),
the Serpent, a creeping thing, is anomalous to the
opposition Man versus Woman.

Christian artists have always been sensitive to this fact; they manage to give the monster a somewhat hermaphrodite appearance while still indicating some kind of identification between the Serpent and Eve herself. Hugo Van der Goes, in 'The Fall' at the Kunsthistorisches Museum, Vienna, puts Eve and the Serpent in the same posture. Michaelangelo makes Adam and Eve both gaze with loving adoration on the Serpent, but the Serpent has Eve's face.[5]

Adam and Eve eat the forbidden fruit and become aware of sexual difference; death becomes inevitable (iii. 3–8). But now for the first time pregnancy and reproduction become possible. Eve does not become pregnant until after she has been expelled from Paradise (iv. 1).

## LOWER BAND

Cain the Gardener and Abel the Herdsman repeat the antithesis between the first three days of the Creation and the last three days in the first story. Abel's living world is more pleasing to God (iv. 4–5). Cain's fratricide compares with Adam's incest and so God's questioning and cursing of Cain (iv. 9–12) has the same form and sequence as God's questioning and cursing of Adam, Eve and the Serpent (ii. 9–19). The latter part of iii. 16 is later repeated exactly (iv. 7), so Cain's sin was not only fratricide but also incestuous homosexuality. In order that immortal monosexual existence in Paradise may be exchanged for fertile heterosexual existence in reality, Cain, like Adam, must acquire a wife (iv. 17). To this end Adam must eliminate a sister: Cain a brother. The symmetry is complete.

The issue here is the logical basis of incest categories and closely analogous patterns must occur in all mythologies regardless of their superficial content.

**Genesis i. 1 – ii. 3 and v. 1–8**

← static world (death) → ← moving world (life) →

| 1 2nd day | 2 3rd day | 3 | 4 4th day | 5 5th day | 6 6th day | 7 |
|---|---|---|---|---|---|---|
| 'waters above' (rain) | | | | | | |
| firmament (sky) | | | | | | |
| 'waters below' (ocean) | land / sea | grass \| cereals \| fruit trees | (life-death alternation) sun (day) \| moon (night) | birds / fish | cattle \| beasts \| 'creeping things' | |
| | | | | | Man and Woman | SETH → ENOS |

**Genesis ii. 4 / Genesis iv. 1**

HEAVEN — MIST → EARTH

trees in the Garden (many): life \| death \| good \| evil

Man in the Garden (alone)

REAL WORLD (divided)

one river becomes four

PARADISE (IDEAL WORLD) a unity

'helpmeets of Man': birds \| cattle \| beasts \| Woman (creeping things)

Man in the Garden (alone)

anomalous category

sex difference denied (unity) — MAN / SERPENT / WOMAN — sex difference admitted (duality)

PARADISE eternal life

COPULATION FORBIDDEN (incest)

EXPULSION

COPULATION ALLOWED

EVE — ADAM — CAIN

REAL WORLD (life and death)

static world given fertility — living world given fertility

Genesis iv, 2–16

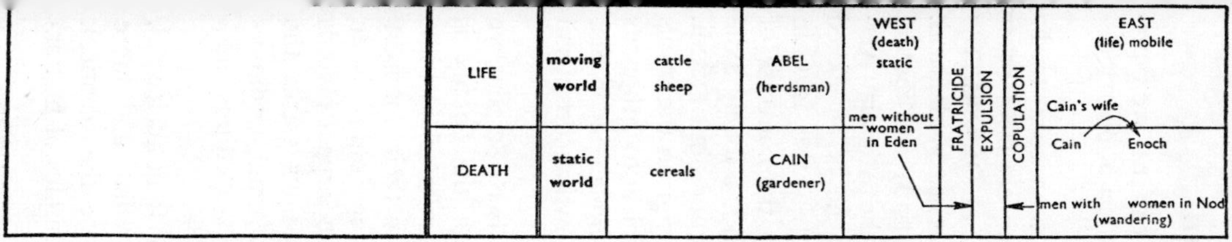

Fig 1 The four chapters of Genesis contain three separate creation stories. Horizontal bands correspond to (a) seven-day creation; (b) Garden of Eden; and (c) Cain and Abel. Each story sets up the opposition Death versus Life, God versus Man. World is 'made alive' by using categories of 'woman' and 'creeping thing' to mediate this opposition

Cross-cultural comparison becomes easier if we represent the analysis as a systematic pattern of binary discriminations as in Fig. 2.

Adam/Eve and Cain/Abel are then seen to be variants of a theme which can also occur in other forms, as in the well-known myth of Oedipus. The actual symbolism in these two cases is nearly identical. Oedipus, like Adam and Cain, is initially earthbound and immobile. The conclusion of the Athenian version of the Oedipus story is that he is an exiled wanderer, protected by the gods. So also is Cain (iv. 14–15). The Bible also includes the converse of this pattern. In Genesis xxviii Jacob is a lonely exile and wanderer under God's protection, but (xxxii. 24–32) he is renamed Israel and thus given the status of a first ancestor with a territorial autochthonous base, and he is tamed by God. Although Jacob dies abroad in Egypt he is buried on his own ancestral soil in Israel (xl. 29–32; l. 5–7).

In the Oedipus story, in place of Eve's Serpent we have Jocasta's Sphinx. Like Jocasta the Sphinx is female, like Jocasta the Sphinx commits suicide, like the Serpent the Sphinx leads men to their doom by verbal cunning, like the Serpent the Sphinx is an anomalous monster. Eve listens to the Serpent's words and betrays Adam into incest; Oedipus solves the Sphinx riddle and is led into incest. Again, Oedipus's patricide replaces Cain's fratricide – Oedipus, incidentally, meets Laius 'at a cross roads'.

Parallels of this kind seem too close to be accidental, but this kind of algebra is unfamiliar and more evidence will be needed to convince the sceptical. Genesis contains several further examples of first ancestors.

Firstly, Noah survived the destruction of the world by flood together with three sons and their wives.

Prior to this the population of the world had included three kinds of being – 'sons of God', 'daughters of men' and 'giants' who were the offspring of the union of the other two (vi. 1–4). Since the forbears of Noah's daughters-in-law have all been destroyed by the Flood, Noah becomes a unique ancestor of all mankind without the implication of incest. Chapter ix. 1–7 addressed to Noah is almost the duplicate of i. 27–30 addressed to Adam.

Though heterosexual incest is evaded, the theme of homosexual incest in the Cain and Abel story recurs in the Noah saga when drunken Noah is seduced by his own son Ham (ix. 21–5). The Canaanites, descendants of Ham, are for this reason accursed. (That a homosexual act is intended is evident from the language 'Ham saw the nakedness of his father'. Compare Leviticus xviii. 6–19, where 'to uncover the nakedness of' consistently means to have sexual relations with.)

In the second place Lot survives the destruction of the world by fire together with two nubile daughters. Drunken Lot is seduced by his own daughters (xix. 30–8). The Moabites and the Ammonites, descendants of these daughters, are for this reason accursed. In chapter xix the men of Sodom endeavour to have homosexual relations with two angels who are visiting Lot. Lot offers his nubile daughters instead but they escape unscathed. The implication is that Lot's incest is less grave than heterosexual relations with a foreigner, and still less grave than homosexual relations.

Thirdly, the affair of the Sodomites and the Angels contains echoes of 'the sons of God' and 'the daughters of men' but links superficially with chapter xviii where Abraham receives a visit from God and two angels who promise that his ageing and barren wife

Sarah shall bear a son. Sarah is Abraham's half-sister by the same father (xx. 12) and his relations with her are unambiguously incestuous (Leviticus xviii. 9). Abraham loans Sarah to Pharaoh saying that she is his sister (xii. 19). He does the same with King Abimelech (xx. 2). Isaac repeats the game with Abimelech (xxvi. 9–11) but with a difference. Isaac's wife Rebekah is his father's brother's son's daughter (second

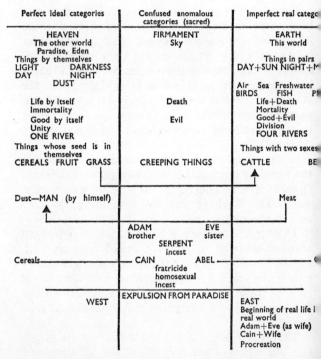

| Perfect ideal categories | Confused anomalous categories (sacred) | Imperfect real catego[ries] |
|---|---|---|
| HEAVEN<br>The other world<br>Paradise, Eden | FIRMAMENT<br>Sky | EARTH<br>This world |
| Things by themselves<br>LIGHT　　DARKNESS<br>DAY　　NIGHT<br>　　DUST | | Things in pairs<br>DAY+SUN　NIGHT+M |
| | | Air　Sea　Freshwater　P[...]<br>BIRDS　FISH　P[...] |
| Life by itself<br>Immortality | Death | Life+Death<br>Mortality |
| Good by itself<br>Unity<br>ONE RIVER | Evil | Good+Evil<br>Division<br>FOUR RIVERS |
| Things whose seed is in themselves<br>CEREALS　FRUIT　GRASS | CREEPING THINGS | Things with two sexes<br>CATTLE　　　　BE |
| Dust—MAN (by himself) | | Meat |
| | ADAM　　　　EVE<br>brother　　　sister<br>　SERPENT<br>　incest | |
| Cereals————— | —CAIN　　　ABEL—<br>fratricide<br>homosexual<br>incest | |
| WEST | EXPULSION FROM PARADISE | EAST<br>Beginning of real life i[n]<br>real world<br>Adam+Eve (as wife)<br>Cain+Wife<br>Procreation |

Fig 2　Incest categories have a logical basis in all myths. Simi[larity] between myths is seen most clearly if they are analysed in a b[locked] form as shown in this table

cousin) and the relation is *not* in fact incestuous. The
barrenness of Sarah is an aspect of her incest. The
supernatural intervention which ultimately ensures
that she shall bear a child is evidence that the incest is
condoned. Pharaoh and Abimelech both suffer supernatural penalties for the lesser offence of adultery,
but Abraham, the incestuous husband, survives
unscathed.

There are other stories in the same set. Hagar,
Sarah's Egyptian slave, bears a son Ishmael to Abraham whose descendants are wanderers of low status.
Sarah's son Isaac is marked out as of higher status
than the sons of Abraham's concubines, who are sent
away to 'the east country' (c.f. wandering Cain who
made his home in Nod 'eastward of Eden'). Isaac
marries a kinswoman in preference to a Canaanite
woman. Esau's marriage to a Hittite woman is marked
as a sin. In contrast his younger and favoured twin
brother Jacob marries two daughters of his mother's
brother who is in turn Jacob's father's father's
brother's son's son.

All in all, this long series of repetitive and inverted
tales asserts:

(a) the overriding virtue of close kin endogamy;
(b) that the sacred hero-ancestor Abraham can carry
this so far that he marries his paternal half-sister (an
incestuous relationship). Abraham is thus likened to
Pharaoh, for the Pharaohs of Egypt regularly married
their paternal half-sisters; and
(c) that a rank order is established which places the
tribal neighbours of the Israelites in varying degrees
of inferior status depending upon the nature of the
defect in their original ancestry as compared with the
pure descent of Jacob (Israel).

The myth requires that the Israelites be descended

unambiguously from Terah the father of Abraham. This is achieved only at the cost of a breach of the incest rule; but by reciting a large number of similar stories which entail even greater breaches of sexual morality the relations of Abraham and Sarah finally stand out as uniquely virtuous. Just as Adam and Eve are virtuous as compared to Cain and Abel, so Abraham's incest can pass unnoticed in the context of such outrageous characters as Ham, Lot's daughters, and the men of Sodom.

I have concentrated here upon the issue of sexual rules and transgressions so as to show how a multiplicity of repetitions, inversions and variations can add up to a consistent 'message'. I do not wish to imply that this is the only structural pattern which these myths contain.

The novelty of the analysis which I have presented does not lie in the facts but in the procedure. Instead of taking each myth as a thing in itself with a 'meaning' peculiar to itself it is assumed, from the start, that every myth is one of a complex and that any pattern which occurs in one myth will recur, in the same or other variations, in other parts of the complex. The structure that is common to all variations becomes apparent when different versions are 'superimposed' one upon the other.

Whenever a corpus of mythology is recited in its religious setting such structural patterns are 'felt' to be present, and convey meaning much as poetry conveys meaning. Even though the ordinary listener is not fully conscious of what has been communicated, the 'message' is there in a quite objective sense. If the labour of programming could be performed the actual analysis could be done by a computer far better than by any human. Furthermore it seems evident that much the same patterns exist in the most diverse kinds of mythology. This seems to me to be a fact of great psychological, sociological and scientific significance. Here truly are observable phenomena which are the expression of unobservable realities.

# THE LEGITIMACY OF SOLOMON
*Some structural aspects of Old Testament history*

I must start with a personal disavowal. This essay employs an explicitly Lévi-Straussian procedure but it is not intended as a guide to wider aspects of Lévi-Strauss thought. Although I feel reasonably safe with Lévi-Strauss's concept of *structure*, I am quite out of my depth when it comes to the related but subtler notion of *esprit*. Lévi-Strauss's *esprit* appears in sundry guises. In 1952, originally in English, he/it was a personalized 'human mind', an uninvited guest who took his place around the conference table among a group of American linguists and anthropologists;[1] in the earlier chapters of *La pensée sauvage* he is perhaps the *bricoleur* – handiman – who is busy contriving culture from the junk of history and anything else that comes to hand;[2] at the conclusion of *Le cru et le cuit*,[3] in more abstract and more serious vein, *esprit* seems to be a kind of limiting characteristic of the human brain mechanism and appears as part of an extremely involved interchange relationship in which it (*esprit*) is the casual force producing myths of which its own structure is a precipitate. Elsewhere again[4] *esprit* seems to correspond to that very mysterious something which is a mediator between 'praxis et pratiques' and which is described as 'le schème conceptuel par l'opération duquel une matière et une forme, dépourvues l'une et l'autre d'existence indépendante, s'accomplissent comme structures, c'est-a-dire comme êtres à la fois

empiriques et intelligibles'. Now although I am en-
tranced by the images which such verbal felicity calls
to mind, I have to confess that, when it comes to the
crunch, I have no clear idea of what it is that Lévi-
Strauss is really talking about. This is my deficiency
not his, but it may be relevant as an answer to poten-
tial critics of this essay. My subject matter here is
also the subject matter of theology, but whereas a
theologian can find in the Old Testament texts a
mystical message which has hermeneutic import for
the whole of humanity, my own analysis reveals only
a patterning of arguments about endogamy and
exogamy, legitimacy and illegitimacy as operative in
the thought processes of Palestinian Jews of the third
century B.C. Perhaps if I had a better understanding
of Lévi-Strauss's *esprit*, which manages to be both
abstract and empirical, particular and universal, all
at the same time, my conclusions might be less thin.
It is the 'larger than life' elements in the schema
which baffle me. If 'John Smith's mind' is only a
'ghost in a machine'[5] at least the machine itself is
concrete and tangible; but 'the human mind' (*l'esprit
humain*) seems to me to be all ghost and no machine,
even when Lévi-Strauss himself expressly disclaims
any metaphysical intention.

Of course the idea that there might be, that indeed
there *must* be, some kind of 'mind' which is in some
sense larger than, exterior to, and independent of any
particular human individual is as old as philosophy
itself. To this category of ideas belong not only
Hegel's *Geist* and Durkheim's 'collective conscience'
but even the basic idea of 'God' itself. All these are
highly contentious terms. In particular, Durkheim's
critics, interpreters and translators constantly dispute
among themselves as to just how far he really intended to reify his concept of a collective person-

ality.[6] Lévi-Strauss's *human mind* seems to me ambiguous in a precisely similiar way.

The relevance of this difficulty for my present essay
is this: I seek to demonstrate the creation of a myth
as the precipitate of the development of an historical
tradition. That myth has characteristics which Lévi-
Strauss considers to be 'caused by' attributes of the
human mind. I do not understand this proposition.

Having, I hope, made my deficiency of understanding clear, let me reaffirm that this essay is intended as
a limited exercise in certain of Lévi-Strauss's methods;
not as an exposition of his theoretical ideas.

Several recent commentators on the work of Lévi-
Strauss have drawn attention to what appears to be
an inconsistency between his theory and his practice.
*La pensée sauvage* is not presented as a peculiarity of
savages but as a fundamental mode of ordering the
world by means of verbal discriminations. There may
be other modes of logic but 'structuralism' is postulated as a universal characteristic of the human
psyche; it should thus manifest itself in every branch
of culture, in all kinds of society, sophisticated as well
as primitive. Yet when Lévi-Strauss comes to demonstrate his method in detail, as in *Les structures élémen-
taires de la parenté* or more recently in *Le cru et le
cuit*, he confines his attention to ultra-primitive
systems for which the ethnographic evidence is
notably thin and the historical record virtually non-
existent. The critics, Paul Ricœur in particular, have
posed the question whether the apparent success of
Lévi-Strauss's method has not depended upon the kinds
of material to which it has been applied. Taking the
particular case of myth interpretation, Ricœur has
noted that although Lévi-Strauss first illustrated his
technique by reference to the Oedipus myth he has

never again committed himself to the interpretation of mythical materials derived from any of the historical societies of Western civilization. All his later and more detailed analyses have been concerned with the myths of a 'totemic' kind from very primitive sources, that is to say mythologies in which there is a notable confusion between human beings and animals but which are characterized by the absence of any setting within an historical chronology, real or imaginary. Ricœur suggests that there may be a fundamental contrast between 'totemic' myths of this kind and the mythologies of civilized peoples. Thus, both in Judaism and in Christianity, the traditional hermeneutic has depended upon an assumption that the Bible itself constitutes a *sacred history*, the chronological axis of which is fundamental. The theologian sees the Bible as a record of the working out of the Divine Will through the processes of history; the significance of the mythological message (the *kerygma*) is inseparable from the recognition that the events occur in a particular historical sequence. Whatever may have been the origin of particular Biblical stories their synthesis has made them into a unity; they are not just a 'collection' of stories, they are stories constituting a sacred history and it is the historical element, the sense of ongoing destiny, that gives the Old Testament its value as a symbol of the unity of the Jewish people.[7] How then does this essential diachrony of the traditional hermeneutic relate to the synchrony of a structural analysis? This is a fair question. Myth proper lacks a chronology in any strict sense, for the beginning and the end must be apprehended simultaneously; significance is to be discerned only in the relations between the component parts of the story; sequence is simply a persistent rearrangement of elements which are present from the start. In this respect a Lévi-Straussian analysis of a myth sequence stands very close to a Freudian analysis of a dream sequence. Curiously enough the events recounted in the mythological tales of Australian aborigines are explicitly described as occurring in 'dream time'; this would be an appropriate description for the temporal context of almost all the mythological stories to which Lévi-Strauss has so far devoted his attention.

In responding to Ricœur's challenge (ibid., pp. 631 ff) Lévi-Strauss has taken the line that prudence requires that we should proceed slowly. The fact that his method has so far been applied to very primitive contexts need not lead us to suppose that it cannot be applied to more sophisticated ones. He notes that, in the Biblical case, the present writer has already demonstrated the existence of Lévi-Straussian structures in the stories which make up the book of Genesis, but Lévi-Strauss himself remains extremely cautious.[8] He advances the rather curious proposition that Old Testament mythology has been 'deformed' by the intellectual operations of Biblical editors and he seems to imply that, on this account, a structural analysis of such materials must prove to be largely a waste of time.

I must confess that I do not fully understand the basis of this argument. Lévi-Strauss's view perhaps links up with his general assumption that a society is a totality of which the essence is embodied in a structure. This structure manifests itself in various forms – e.g. in myth, ritual, rules of marriage, law, etc. Structures of this kind vary both geographically through space and chronologically through time. One structure changes into an adjacent structure by dialectical variation of its component elements. These dialectical variations of a particular structural pattern will ordinarily be distributed through time and space in a random manner. If then the structure embodies a 'message' it is not a message consciously devised by any particular individual but rather a precipitate of the whole system. Conversely any decoding (or interpretation) of the structural pattern will (paradoxically) be dependent upon a random distribution of the more superficially meaningful elements in the system. This argument, which perhaps seems absurd when thus compressed, is in accordance with basic principles in communication theory which have long since been fully assimilated into the doctrines of general linguistics (see also p. 47 and n. 15).

When Lévi-Strauss says that the Biblical texts have been 'deformed' he presumably means that the intellectual operations of the Biblical compilers have operated in conflict with the randomized non-intellectual workings of the structure of ancient Jewish culture, thus making the latter indecipherable.

But I think that Lévi-Strauss would also reject a structuralist interpretation of Biblical materials on other grounds. In structuralist analysis, the elements of a myth (the 'symbols') never have any intrinsic meaning. An element has significance only because of its position in the overall structure in relation to the other elements of the set. Thus we may compare one myth with another and note the varying positions and mutual relations of the various elements concerned but we cannot go further than this without referring back to the total ethnographic context to which the myth refers. In the case of ancient Judaism, Lévi-Strauss affirms that 'le contexte ethnographique fait presque entièrement défaut'. This seems to me something of an exaggeration; Lévi-Strauss has shown no hesitation about applying structuralist analysis to the myths of the Tsimshian and the Bororo, peoples of

whom our ethnographic knowledge is sketchy to say
the least. No doubt our knowledge of Ancient Judaea
is very unsatisfactory, but it is far from non-existent.
In short, I consider Lévi-Strauss's attitude too cautious,
but it needs to be borne in mind that in the remainder
of this essay I am engaged in an enterprise for which
Lévi-Strauss himself has shown no enthusiasm.

What then is my theme? My purpose is to demonstrate that the Biblical story of the succession of
Solomon to the throne of Israel is a myth which
'mediates' a major contradiction. The Old Testament
as a whole asserts that the Jewish political title to the
land of Palestine is a direct gift from God to the descendants of Israel (Jacob). This provides the fundamental basis for Jewish endogamy – the Jews should
be a people of pure blood and pure religion, living in
isolation in their Promised Land. But interwoven with
this theological dogma there is a less idealized form of
tradition which represents the population of ancient
Palestine as a mixture of many peoples over whom the
Jews have asserted political dominance by right of
conquest. The Jews and their 'foreign' neighbours
intermarry freely. The synthesis achieved by the story
of Solomon is such that by a kind of dramatic trick
the reader is persuaded that the second of these des-
criptions, which is morally bad, exemplifies the first
description, which is morally good. My demonstration
is a long and devious one, and the reader must be
patient if I offer a number of minor distractions on
the way.

First a word about method. My quotations come
exclusively from the English language Authorized
Version of the Bible dated 1611. While purists may
object to such a source it has the advantage of easy

verification. I have cross-checked the quotations by reference to more recent English language translations and also by following through the originals as glossed in a variety of standard Biblical commentaries. Since every word, indeed every letter, of the Hebrew text has provided occasion for scholarly dispute I cannot pretend to one hundred per cent accuracy but I do not think that this deficiency is of great significance. Only once or twice does my argument hang upon a point of linguistic detail. For the most part I am concerned with stories not with texts, and for this purpose the long-established English version is good enough.[9]

There is of course an enormous and vastly erudite critical literature which relies on the original Hebrew and purports to sift the historical facts from the legendary accretions and editorial glosses. I am fully aware that many histories of Ancient Israel have been written which treat of the matter as if the facts were as fully and precisely known as, say, the history of England since 1066. In the present essay I am not concerned to challenge the validity of any particular interpretation of this kind though I suspect that my anthropological experience does give me certain advantages over scholars of a more orthodox sort. The original authors and editors of the Biblical texts were obviously intensely interested in the 'history' of the Jewish people, but history is a malleable concept. We cannot know for certain just how the Palestinian Jews of the fourth century B.C. thought about their past, but their historiography is more likely to have resembled that of modern tribal societies than that of nineteenth-century Europeans. Philo and Josephus, who were both orthodox Jews of sophisticated Hellenic culture living in the first century A.D., could both combine an intense respect for the Scriptures with a recognition that they were incredible. Philo interpreted the incredibility as 'allegory'; Josephus re-wrote the texts in paraphrase so as to make the history seem more plausible, and on that account has been condemned by modern Christians for tampering with the 'true history' of the sacred texts! The real point is that Josephus understood very well that what Greek and Roman intellectuals of his time understood by 'true' history was something quite different from the history of the Scriptures. We too can safely accept this insight.

But in fact the usefulness or otherwise of my present paper does not depend at all upon whether any parti-cular interpretation of the Old Testament is true or false considered as historiography, nor does it matter whether any particular interpretation is good or bad theology, Jewish or Christian. My concern is with patterns or structures in the record as we now have it, and this record has been substantially unchanged over a very long period. *Hamlet* remains the same play whatever kind of hash the critics choose to make of it, and the stories of the Old Testament retain the same structures despite all the changing fashions in theol-ogy. To assess these structures we do not need to know how particular stories came to assume their pre-sent form nor the dates at which they were written. Nevertheless the structuralist does make certain special assumptions about the nature of his materials and these need to be emphasized.

Firstly, two points of agreement. All scholarly opinion recognizes that the present recension of the books of the Old Testament is an assemblage of very varied writings which was finally edited and made fully canonical only around 100 B.C.[10] Likewise all agree that the purportedly 'early' works in the col-lection contain numerous interpolations which have been inserted from time to time by later editors in the interests of consistency or with a view to providing traditional support for a disputed point of political or religious doctrine. But orthodox scholarship assumes that from the time of David onwards the individual characters in Biblical stories were 'real people', that is to say they had genuine flesh and blood historical existence, and that even for earlier periods there is a substratum of genuine historical fact. In that case the historian's task is to distinguish this historical reality from the accretions of legend and editorial modification. Thus if two Biblical stories refer to individuals or places of the same name (or very similar names) in different contexts of time and place the *historian* will assume that two quite different 'real entities' are to be distinguished. For the *structuralist* on the other hand the fact that the same name crops up in two different places is of significance in itself in that it suggests a link between the two stories. He is then immediately led to consider whether or not the two stories are associated in other ways also. This is especially relevant in the present case since the duplication of Biblical names is relatively infrequent.

In this respect the structuralist anthropologist is much closer to the theologian than is the orthodox historian. For an historian, every event is unique in itself and two events which occur at different points in chronological time or at different places on the map can never in any sense be 'the same'. But in theological hermeneutic it is commonly assumed that an event reported as having occurred at time/place A can, in some sense, be predictive of another later event occurring at time/place B. Event B is felt to be somehow a *repetition* of Event A. Now this is a very 'mythological' way of treating reality and it is one to which the methods of structuralism are well adapted.

Judged by nineteenth- and twentieth-century conventions a structuralist's approach to Biblical materials is unorthodox but it is not in fact a novelty. On the contrary, the general principle has been recognized for millennia. It could hardly be otherwise. After all, if it really be the case that the 'message' contained in a myth or in a set of myths is communicated through the structure, then it would be astonishing if 2,000 years of intensive Biblical scholarship had not gained some inkling of this fact! If on the other hand structural analysis of Biblical materials were now to reveal 'messages' which are *not* in some degree already known, then we should have good grounds for supposing that the whole business is an accidental triviality. But this is not the case. For example, to start at the very beginning, the structure of the first chapter of Genesis is so obvious that it has been commented upon by Rabbinical authors from the earliest times. The pattern may be summarized as follows: the six days of the Creation form two separate sequences; the first three days are concerned with a static world devoid of life, and the second three days with a moving world of 'living' things; day four is paired with day one, five with two, and six with three.[11] The Rabbinical view has been that the structure of itself embodies a complex theological message. A version of this doctrine was quite recently propounded by Professor Leo Strauss (Chicago) in the following terms:

It seems then that the sequence of creation in the first chapter of the Bible can be stated as follows: from the principle of separation, light; via something which separates, heaven; to something which is separated, earth and sea; to things which are productive of separated things, trees, for

example; then things which can separate themselves from their courses, brutes; and finally a
being which can separate itself from its way,
the right way. I repeat, the clue to the first
chapter seems to be the fact that the account of
the creation consists of two main parts. This implies that the created world is conceived to be
characterized by a fundamental dualism: things
which are different from each other without
having the capacity of local motion and things
which in addition to being different from each
other do have the capacity for local motion. This
means the first chapter seems to be based on the
assumption that the fundamental dualism is that
of distinctness, otherness, as Plato would say,
and of local motion.[12]

From this Professor Strauss goes on to argue that:
'The terrestial living things are either not created in
the image of God – brutes; or in the image of God –
man.' Nature versus Culture! Such arguments in
work which has nothing to do with the school of Lévi-
Strauss show that we should not regard structure and
hermeneutic as intrinsically opposed.

Before I proceed further I must be sure that the
reader fully understands the difference between comparison in terms of content and comparison in terms
of structure. Comparison in terms of content is the
orthodox and obvious technique of 'the comparative
method in anthropology' as practised by Tylor, Frazer,
Westermarck, Briffault and other scholars of the late
nineteenth and early twentieth centuries. Frazer's
three-volume *Folklore in the Old Testament* (1918–
22) exhibits the method on a grand scale; but in the
case of Biblical materials this type of exegesis dates

back to the earliest times: when the author of Matthew i. 23, quotes a passage from Isaiah to validate the truth of his story of the Virgin Birth, he is simply comparing two stories of similar content. In general, the whole hermeneutic argument which represents the New Testament as a fulfilment of the Old, or the Books of Kings as a fulfilment of the warnings of Deuteronomy, depends upon such comparisons.

In contrast, structural analysis leads to the recognition of relationships of a more abstract kind which may associate bodies or material which have little or no similarity of content. A good example is provided by a comparison between the Biblical accounts of (*a*) the sacrifice of Jepthah's daughter and (*b*) the non-sacrifice of Abraham's son. Except that both stories are about 'sacrifice' the similarity of content is very slight.

The following is a summary of Judges xi. 30–40:

(*a*) Jepthah, the Gileadite, makes a vow to make a burnt offering to God if he is granted victory.

(*b*) God grants Jepthah victory.

(*c*) (By implication Jepthah plans to sacrifice an animal or a slave in fulfilment of his vow.)

(*d*) God, in the form of chance, imposes a substitution whereby Jepthah is made to sacrifice his only child, a virgin daughter.

*Outcome*

Jepthah has no descendants of any kind.

The following is a corresponding analysis of Genesis xxii. 1–18.

(*d*) God requires Abraham to sacrifice his only son Isaac as evidence of faith and obedience.

(*c*) As Abraham prepares to obey, God imposes a

substitution whereby Abraham in fact sacrifices an animal in fulfilment of his duty.

(*b*) Abraham thus demonstrates his faith and obedience.

(*a*) God makes a vow that Abraham shall have countless descendants.

*Outcome*

All the children of Israel claim descent from Abraham.

When presented in this way the two stories appear as mirror images of each other. 'God' is changed to 'father', 'father' is changed to 'God'; 'virgin daughter' is changed to 'virgin son'; the sequence represented by the clauses (*a*), (*b*), (*c*), (*d*) in the first story is exactly reversed in the second story. The mythical outcome of the first story 'the father has no descendants' is the exact opposite to the mythical outcome of the second 'the father has countless descendants'. It can thus be said that these two stories have an identical structure, since the second can be produced from the first by the simplest possible transformation rule: 'Substitute for each element its binary opposite.'

One of the main arguments which Lévi-Strauss advances in his studies of myth proper is that the repetitions which are so characteristic of all forms of folklore are significant not so much because of their similarity as because of their differences. In Lévi-Strauss's view myths commonly focus around some irresolvable paradox of logic or of fact: e.g. 'How could there be a first man and a first woman who were not also brother and sister?', 'How can one fit a desire for immortality with a knowledge of the certainty of impending death?', 'How is it that human beings are on the one hand animals (natural) and on the other hand not-animals (cultural)?' The 'variations on a theme' which constantly recur in mythological systems serve to blur the edges of such 'contradictions' and thus to remove them from immediate consciousness.

If we treat the material selectively without reference to the chronological (historical) dimension then there are many sets of Biblical stories which conform to this principle of Lévi-Straussian analysis. I have cited some examples of this in earlier papers (Leach 1961; 1962).[8] Another such set is provided by the stories of Dinah (Genesis xxxiv), Abimelech (Judges ix), Jepthah (Judges xi. 1–11), Samson (Judges xiii–xvi). Here the common theme is a 'contradiction' which is the historical torment of all religious sects which acquire political ambitions but which has been of particular significance in Jewish history from the earliest times right down to the present day. On the one hand the practice of sectarian endogamy is essential to maintain the purity of the faith, on the other hand exogamous marriages may be politically expedient if peaceful relations are to be maintained with hostile neighbours.

In a formal sense the Biblical texts consistently affirm the righteousness of endogamy and the sinfulness of exogamy, but the structural 'message' keeps harking back to the 'contradiction'. Thus:

(1) The Dinah story affirms unambiguously the sinfulness of allowing an Israelite girl to cohabit with a foreigner (in this case a Shechemite-Canaanite) even if the foreigner is prepared to adopt the Israelite faith. But the story points out that the enforcement of this principle must lead to political difficulties.

(2) Abimelech is a half-blood Israelite-Shechemite by a Shechemite mother. On the death of his father he

joins his mother's people, kills all his pure-blooded half-brothers except one, and is himself killed.

(3) Jepthah is also a half-blood Israelite by a foreign mother. On the death of his father he is chased away by his father's people but eventually called back to be their leader. His pure-blooded relatives are thereby saved but his only daughter is sacrificed and he dies without descendants.

(4) Samson is a pure-blooded Israelite hero who has a series of sexual liaisons with foreign (Philistine) women interspersed with battles against Philistine men. The women are consistently treacherous and finally bring about his downfall. The treachery of the foreign women is here the counterpart of the dishonourableness of the foreign men in the Dinah story.

The stories form a 'set' but it is not a 'closed set'; they associate also with an indefinitely large number of other stories. It will be seen that the Dinah and Samson stories are 'opposites' and the Abimelech and Jepthah stories are 'opposites', but the Dinah and Abimelech stories are linked through the reference to Shechem. Both the latter imply that the 'King of Shechem' is a foreigner. But this is a very critical issue which leads much further afield, for Jeroboam was 'King of Shechem' and the foreignness or non-foreignness of Jeroboam is a matter of major import (see p. 51). The reader should take particular note of the way in which in these stories the moral issue of the legitimacy of sex relations is intertwined with the political issue of 'How foreign is a foreigner?'

But what, it may be asked, is the merit of such structural comparison? Even if the similarity of pattern be conceded what does this tell us? To this question I can offer no simple answer. To some extent the pleasure which can be derived from structural analysis is aesthetic. Just as a mathematician feels that an elegant solution is 'better' than a clumsy solution to the same problem, so the merit of 'structuralism' cannot be narrowly judged by any such practical criterion as: 'Does this line of investigation lead to any useful result?' A demonstration of the elegance of the 'unconscious operations of the human mind' has merit in itself, even if some of us may feel uncertain as to just what kind of an operating agent this 'human mind' may be.

But if practical justification is needed, I would put it this way. At the very least the discovery of a consistent structural pattern in a set of ethnographic data leads us to compare what otherwise seems incomparable and invites further questions of a new kind at a different more concrete level of ethnography. I have not the space to develop this point but I can indicate what I mean. Jepthah's daughter is said to have been sacrificed at a place called Mizpah which was the locale for a four-day annual festival attended by unmarried girls (seeking husbands?) (Judges xi. 34–40). The non-sacrifice of Isaac took place on Mount Moriah which is the site of the temple at Jerusalem (Genesis xxii. 2; 2 Chronicles iii. 1). Strict attention to geographical detail suggests that there are at least two different places described as Mizpah in Old Testament texts but structural considerations would now lead us to consider whether they have anything in common and also whether they stand associated with Jerusalem in any other way than by a simple inversion of mythology.

But I must confine myself to a narrower theme, the structural analysis of chronological sequences. Let us return to the point made by Ricœur that the text of the Bible, as we have it, is a chronological history and not a timeless myth. How does this affect the argument?

The facts are plain enough. Apart from the manuals of tribal law and custom and the sermons of the prophets, the main body of the Old Testament is presented as if it were a history of the Jewish people from the Creation down to the time of Ezra and Nehemiah. It is also plain that source materials of very different kinds have been brought together and synthesized, by skilful and perhaps repeated editing, into a single story. That in itself is not remarkable.

Much the same might be said of any kind of history book, whether the history in question be true, false or purely imaginary. An indefinitely large number of events have actually occurred in the past. Only a tiny selection of these events can ever come to be perpetuated as 'history'. The process by which the selection is made is a complex combination of pure accident and editorial interest, but the net result is quite arbitrary. Political events get worked into the historical records because literate people everywhere seem to have a persistent belief in the 'importance' of politics. But this is only a value judgment and if the chroniclers of ancient kingdoms had happened to write about other matters we should not now find their stories less interesting. Of 'history' as of 'myth', it is quite sensible for the sociological inquirer to ask himself: 'Why does this particular incident (rather than some other) occur in the story in this particular form (rather than in some other)?' It is not sufficient to give the orthodox historian's answer which is: 'Well that is what really happened', for many other things also really happened which do not appear in the story at all.

The structuralist has a special kind of answer to this kind of question. He argues that the significance of individual items in any kind of story is to be found in their patterned arrangement. What attracts his attention is not the content of any particular story but the contrast of pattern as between one story and another. This principle should be just as applicable to stories which purport to be 'history' as to stories which are palpably 'myth'.

Any honest man who writes or edits a history believes that what he writes is true, and in the case of a religious history he may well believe that in displaying this truth he is inspired by God. But clearly he cannot believe that what he writes is the *whole* truth. What he records as the truth is only that part of the totality of things which *he* considers 'important', and it is plain that what constitutes historical importance can vary very greatly both from place to place and from time to time. It is surely a commonplace that to understand any particular history book we first need to understand something about the particular interests and orientation of the latest editor. Editors are not authors. Most editors have a great respect for the texts with which they have to deal (and this perhaps is especially true of priestly editors of religious texts) but, even so, the rearrangements, glosses and emendations which any editor makes necessarily reflect the special attitudes of his own time rather than the attitudes and intentions of his predecessors.

Viewed in this rather special way, as a much edited history book, the Old Testament must be regarded as a compilation of ancient and modern documents finally brought together by editors who shared the general attitudes of the authors of the Books of Nehemiah and Ezra.[13] What this attitude may have been was perceptively assessed by S. A. Cook nearly forty years ago:

With Nehemiah and Ezra we enter upon the era of normative Judaism. Judah was a religious community whose representative was the high priest of Jerusalem. Instead of sacerdotal kings, there were royal priests anointed with oil, arrayed with kingly insignia, claiming the usual kingly dues in addition to the customary rights of priests. With his priests and Levites and with the chiefs and nobles of the Jewish families, the high priest directs this small state [...] This hierarchical government can find no foundation in the Hebrew monarchy.[14]

It is in accord with the needs of such a society as this that the text of the Old Testament as a whole (as we now have it) sets the mark of approval on orderly government of a monarchical kind while disapproving of all individual monarchs. It is consistent that it should lay stress upon the unique importance of Jerusalem as the cult centre of the Jewish faith in which the tribe of Judah stands for the secular arm and that of Levi for the spiritual, and it is quite appropriate that the tone of Nehemiah and Ezra should be one of bigoted sectarianism which demands above all else that Jews shall separate themselves off sharply from all foreigners and that there shall be no intermarriage between Jew and Gentile. For Nehemiah and Ezra such intermarriage is the sin of sins. Yet this doctrine of exclusiveness leads to contradiction.

Whatever the predominant party might think of foreign marriages, the tradition of the half-Moabite origin of David serves [...] to emphasize the debt which Judah and Jerusalem owed to one of its neighbours [...] Again, although some desired a self-contained community opposed to the heathen neighbours of Jerusalem the story of

Jonah implicitly contends against the attempt of Judaism to close its doors. The conflicting tendencies were incompatible [...]*

It is with precisely these incompatibilities that this essay is primarily concerned.

Here I must emphasize the very important distinction between structural contradiction (large-scale incompatibility of implication) and content contradiction (inconsistencies in the small-scale details of textual assertion). Contradictions of the latter kind abound. Mostly they are probably a by-product of editorial glosses originally introduced with the purpose of eliminating still more glaring contradictions. It is precisely the all-pervasiveness and random incidence of such inconsistency which makes these 'historical' texts appropriate material for structural analysis, for, under these randomized conditions, the underlying structure of the story ceases to be under the rational control of the editors and generates a momentum of its own.[15] At this point the story ceases to be simply a chronicle of events, it becomes a drama.

Ordinary modern readers are unlikely to pay close attention to Biblical genealogies or to recognize the variety of inconsistencies which these contain. The details are tedious, yet since I claim that it is the randomness of inconsistency which justifies the application of structural analysis I must at least exemplify what I mean.

In the remainder of this section I try to show how the editorial amendments of various hands have become woven into an involuted network which can convey a 'message' which was not necessarily consciously intended by any particular editor.

*Cook, op. cit.

45

An explicit logical basis for the obsessional stress on endogamy which is so evident in Nehemiah and Ezra is provided by 1 Kings xi. 1–8. Solomon the wise, the great king, the builder of the temple, nevertheless is a sinner in that he 'loved many strange women, together with the daughter of Pharaoh, women of the Moabites, Ammonites, Edomites, Zidonians and Hittites.' As a consequence 'did Solomon build an high place for Chemosh, the abomination of Moab, in the hill that is before Jerusalem and for Molech the abomination of the children of Ammon, and likewise did he for all his strange wives, which burnt incense and sacrificed unto their gods'. The inference is that if the Israelites would only keep to the rules and marry only with women of their own kind then they would not be led astray by their foreign wives! The practical difficulty is to decide just who is or who is not a foreign wife.

Taken at its face value, the text of the Old Testament represents the relation between the various tribal groups involved as one of binary segmentation of the most consistent kind. The skeleton genealogy of Figure 1 is exactly comparable to dozens of diagrams discussed in contemporary works by British social anthropologists.[16] A traditional genealogy of this kind serves to discriminate very precisely the exact 'degree of foreignness' which separates one group from another. Thus from the viewpoint of members of the tribe of Judah, the hierarchy of social distance should be: (1) Fellow members of the tribe (lineage) of Judah; (2) Other tribes descended from Leah; (3) Tribes descended from Zilpah; (4) The tribe of Benjamin; (5) Tribes descended from Joseph; (6) Tribes descended from Bilhah; (7) Edomites; (8) Ishmaelites; (9) Moabites and Ammonites; (10) Canaanites; (11) Other Gentiles; (12) Kenites. Biblical texts, notably

Joshua xiv–xxii, also specify very precisely just which territorial areas within the Promised Land are to be regarded as the hereditary land of each tribal segment.

This territorial allocation is simpler than might at first appear for the whole of the southern area, which is later treated as the 'Kingdom of Judah', is primarily allocated to Judah (with the Calebites and the tribe of Simeon as intrusive elements) while correspondingly the whole of the northern area, which is later treated as the 'Kingdom of Israel' (and is roughly equivalent to the historical Samaria), is allocated to the descendants of Joseph (Ephraim, Manasseh). Benjamin receives a narrow strip dividing these two main blocks while the other Israelite tribes are distributed in a ring around the north and east. The heart of the matter is thus treated as a segmentary opposition between the descendants of Leah (i.e. Judah) and the descendants of Rachel (i.e. Ephraim, Manasseh, Benjamin) but with Benjamin both territorially and genealogically in a somewhat equivocal position 'in the middle'[17] (see Figure 2).

But squaring this ideal pattern with the practical realities must at all times have been very difficult. The tribal composition of the Palestinian population was not tidily distributed. Even in the capital city itself 'the Jebusites [Canaanites] dwell with the children of Judah at Jerusalem unto this day' (Joshua xv. 63). Hebron, the reputed site of Abraham's tomb where David ruled for seven years, is specified as the hereditary territory of Caleb the Kenazite (Edomite) with the gloss that it had formerly belonged to the children of Heth (Canaanites) (Joshua xv. 14; Genesis xxxvi. 9–11; Genesis xxiii. 17–20). Even the formal rule book (Deuteronomy xxiii) equivocates about just how foreign is a foreigner. Edomites (and more surprisingly Egyptians) are not to be abhorred. 'The children that

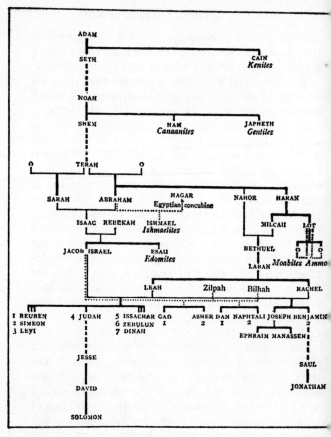

Fig 1 Skeleton Genealogy

NOTES: (i) Sarah, Abraham's half-sister has the status of wife. Ha[gar]
the Egyptian is bond-servant to Sarah and concubine to Abraham.

(ii) Leah and Rachel are full sisters and kin to Jacob through [both]
parents. Zilpah is bond-servant to Leah; Bilhah is bond-servant [to]
Rachel.

(iii) Benjamin is the youngest child of Jacob-Israel. Rachel dies at [his]
birth. He is the only one of the children to be born within [the]
confines of the territory later allocated to his descendants (see Fig [2]).
The name Benjamin means 'son of the right hand'.

(iv) Esau and Jacob are twins. Esau is the elder but he sells his bi[rth]
right to Jacob. In sharp contrast to Jacob, Esau's wives are all Cann[aan]-
ites (Genesis xxxvi).

are begotten of them shall enter into the congregation of the Lord in their third generation.' Ammonites
and Moabites on the other hand are absolutely tainted
'even to their tenth generation shall they not enter
into the congregation of the Lord for ever.' Thus, even
for the Patriarchs the distinction Israelite/Foreigner
was not a clear-cut matter of black and white but a
tapering off through various shades of grey. The
reason for this must be sought in later circumstance.
The Jewish sectarians of the late historical Jerusalem
were surrounded not only by foreigners, who were un-
qualified heathen, but also by semi-foreigners, such
as the Samaritans who claimed to be Israelites like
themselves. How strictly should the rules of endogamy apply in such cases?

The same kind of ambiguity is to be found woven
into seemingly quite straightforward historical traditions. 'History' tells us of two Israelite kingdoms, one
in the south (the Kingdom of Judah), one in the north
(the Kingdom of Israel).

This at once poses a contradiction. The children of
Israel should be one people not two. Are the
Northerners real Israelites or foreigners? The text
equivocates. Individually most of the kings in both
kingdoms are represented as evil men, but the kings
of Israel are more evil than the others and they are
evil in a special way; with monotonous regularity they
'walk in the way of Jeroboam and his sin wherewith
he made Israel to sin'. This particular sin is specified
at 1 Kings xii. 25–35; it lies in the fact that he recognizes holy places other than Jerusalem. Consistent
with this there is a recurrent tendency to treat the
Northerners as altogether heathen. This finds its purest
expression in the story of Ahab, King of Israel, who is
a 'bad guy' in every possible respect. To rub this point
home Ahab is made the contemporary of Jehoshaphat,

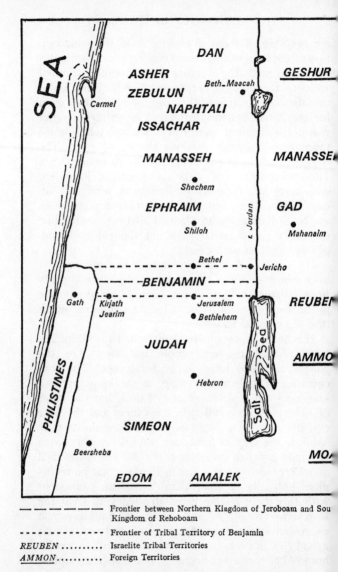

Fig 2 Schematic Map of Old Testament Palestine

| | |
|---|---|
| ————————— | Frontier between Northern Kingdom of Jeroboam and Sou Kingdom of Rehoboam |
| - - - - - - - - - - - | Frontier of Tribal Territory of Benjamin |
| *REUBEN* .......... | Israelite Tribal Territories |
| *AMMON* ........... | Foreign Territories |

King of Judah, who is a 'good guy' in every possible respect. Then precisely at this point where the issue seems to have become clear-cut – Good Southerners (us)/Bad Northerners (foreigners) – the whole issue is compromised. The royal house of Judah and the royal house of Israel (Samaria) become allied by marriage and maintain the alliance over several generations.

These marriages are treated as legitimate marriages, which implies that in *this* context the Northerners are, after all, proper Israelites and legitimate members of the faith! So the Northern Kingdom is a legitimate foundation? But to admit this would contradict the doctrine of the unique legitimacy of the royal house of Judah and the unitary ascendancy of Solomon and Jerusalem. The existence of the dual kingdom is itself a paradox. Its foundation is represented as the result of a revolt by the Northerner JEROBOAM against the legitimate Southerner REHOBOAM. (The mythical nature of the 'historical' characters is shown by the fact that the former name is derived from the latter by a phonetic reversal of the first syllable.)* However, although Jeroboam is a usurper, a secessionist and a heretic, he nevertheless seems to be granted a kind of spurious legitimacy. He is rather carefully distinguished as

Jeroboam the son of Nebat an Ephrathite of Zereda, Solomon's servant, whose mother was Zeruah, a widow [...] Solomon made him ruler over all the charge of the house of Joseph (1 Kings xi. 26–8).

Observe that it is Solomon himself who sets up Jeroboam as ruler over the northern part of the kingdom. Jeroboam stands to Solomon as Joseph to Pharaoh. But this is ambiguous for while Joseph was

* In Hebrew the phonetic inversion is more complex than in the English translation.

undeniably the servant of Pharaoh it was Joseph not Pharaoh who was favoured by God. Then again, the name of Jeroboam's mother reads like a pun. The word means 'leprous', which might be appropriate if the emphasis were on Jeroboam's illegitimate status. But perhaps we should also read Zeruiah[18] which would make Jeroboam a half-brother to Joab and a sister's son to King David (1 Chronicles ii. 16)! Jeroboam's status as a man of Zereda would imply that he was a metalworker (2 Chronicles iv. 17) which in turn indicates a 'middle of the road' position (see p. 60). Finally Jeroboam is specified as one of the lineage of Ephrath, so the position of Ephrath in the genealogy should determine whether or not he can in any sense be of the blood royal. As it turns out the genealogies are strikingly inconsistent on precisely this point.

1 Chronicles ii alone contains several distinguishable doctrines. At v. 9 Caleb (Chelubai) is one of three sons of Hezron, a grandson of Judah. Salma (Salmon) and the line of Jesse to David descends from Caleb's brother Ram. However at vv. 19, 50, 51 Ephrath is Caleb's wife. From her descends a lineage which includes Salma and the men of Bethlehem. At v. 24 Caleb-Ephrath is a place. Genesis xxxv. 19, indentifies this place as Bethlehem the birthplace of *Benjamin* and the burial-place of Rachel, but Ruth i. 2, with equal assurance, identifies Ephrath as Bethlehem-*Judah* the ancestral home of Boaz and the House of Jesse. 1 Chronicles iv. 1–4, has Ephrath again the wife of Carmi (Chelubai : Caleb) who is a son of Hezron and ancestor of the men of Bethlehem, but vv. 11–16 go on to discuss the descendants of 'Caleb the son of Jephunneh', the Kenazite (Edomite) hero of Numbers xxxii. 12, and Joshua xv. 13.

Close pursuit of this jumble of alternatives merely

leads to more and more confusion, but in the end there is a kind of pattern to it : (a) the ancestral Caleb is simultaneously both a marginal foreigner (Edomite) and also an ultra devout member of the faith who carries the principle of endogamy to its legal limits by marrying off his daughter to his own younger brother (Joshua xv. 13–17). (b) He is alternatively associated with Judah and with Benjamin, with Rehoboam through Jesse and with Jeroboam through Ephrath, or with both at once. (c) He is Lord of Hebron, which is David's city before the establishment of Jerusalem; but he is also not Lord of Hebron, since Hebron belongs to the Kohathites, a lineage of Levi (Joshua xxi. 10–12). But this too is a contradiction since the Levites received no inheritance (Joshua xiii. 14).

There is this much consistency at least : whatever is asserted about Caleb and/or Ephrath, the exact opposite is also asserted.

The reader need not try to digest all these details. The crux of the matter is quite simple; let me repeat : any attempt to synthesize into a unitary whole a set of stories which purport to provide historical justification for rival political positions must end up as a text full of paradoxical contradictions. The received text of the Old Testament abounds with such contradictions, and the final result is a 'history' of randomized incidents with the structure of 'myth'. What the myth then 'says' is not what the editors consciously intended to say but rather something which lies deeply embedded in Jewish traditional culture as a whole.

However we may choose to distinguish between Old Testament history and Old Testament myth, myth and history alike must serve mythical functions. Both must serve to justify the doctrine that the Israelites

are the divinely ordained owners of the whole promised land from Dan to Beersheba, both must also
justify the doctrine that the Israelites, a people of
common descent, form an exclusive religious sect, and
both doctrines need to be fitted in with the tradition of
the dual monarchy and with the empirical fact that
the land in question has a very mixed population in
which the Israelites, narrowly defined, are a minority
not in full political control. In any strictly logical
sense the facts and the politico-religious theories are
not mutually compatible as we can easily see if we
transfer the argument to its modern setting: Jews
cannot assimilate themselves fully into the nations of
which they are a part while at the same time main-
taining a narrow religious sectarianism which abhors
every kind of social contact between Jew and non-
Jew.

In the Biblical texts this fundamental contradiction is glossed over by offering repeated partial, yet
contradictory, 'solutions'. The problem is not resolved
because it is irresolvable, yet it seems to be resolved.
Lévi-Strauss has made the same point in his studies of
myth. Myths serve to provide an apparent resolution,
or 'mediation', of problems which are by their very
nature incapable of any final resolution. It will help
to clarify later sections of this paper if we now reduce
the foregoing Biblical contradiction to an elementary
universalistic formula and if we also prejudge the
issue of indicating where the analysis is going to lead
to:

(a) a taboo against incest coupled with a rule of exogamy provides a basis for forming marriage alliances
between antagonistic groups within a single political
community. Further, it is the nature of real political
communities that they consist of self-discriminated

groups which are at any point in time either mutually antagonistic or in alliance.

(b) a rule of endogamy provides a basis for expressing the unitary solidarity of a religious community, the chosen people of God. In real life religious communities and political communities seldom coincide. There is a near incompatibility between a rule of endogamy and a taboo against incest. There is a total incompatibility between a rule of endogamy and the recognition that society consists of potentially antagonistic groups allied by marriage.

(c) The final editors of the Biblical texts were members of an established Jewish church whose members thought of themselves as the direct successors to the House of Judah (as manifested in David) and of the Kingdom of Judah (as governed by Rehoboam and his successors). In polar opposition to the Jewish church stands the world of the Gentiles. In polar opposition to David and Rehoboam stand Foreigners (as exemplified by, e.g., Philistines). But just as in the real world there were intermediate categories such as Samaritans who were neither Jew nor Gentile, so also traditional 'history' provided intermediate categories, 'the descendants of Rachel', 'the House of Joseph', 'the tribe of Benjamin', 'the Kingdom of Jeroboam', 'the Calebites', 'the Edomites'. It is in the ambiguities of the relations between the Men of Judah and these other historical-legendary-mythical peoples that we see the 'resolution' of the endogamy/exogamy incompatibility described above.

A structural analysis requires us to distinguish a 'set' of stories and to display the structures which are common to the set. The Old Testament contains a very great number of distinguishable stories and since they are certainly, from one point of view, all members of a single set, a *full* structural analysis would need to tie *all* these stories together. My present objective is much more limited. I merely wish to show that the chronological sequence in Biblical history may itself have 'structural' relevance. For this purpose I need only to distinguish a suitable subset of stories which is likely to prove amenable to partial analysis. Where we start is somewhat arbitrary, so let me pose a problem:

What was the legal basis of Solomon's kingship over the whole land of Israel?

At first sight Solomon's title derives by right of military conquest backed by the strong arm of God. But closer inspection shows that, in the Biblical context, conquest does not provide a legitimate basis for lordship over land. The Israelites themselves are repeatedly the victims of conquest and deportation but this has no effect at all on their land title. Their title derives from God's promise to Abraham as specified in Genesis xvii. 8: 'And I will give unto thee, to thy seed after thee the land wherein thou art a stranger, all the land of Canaan, for an everlasting possession.'

Here is the first inconsistency. Land which the Israelites conquer from strangers can apparently become an inalienable everlasting possession: land which strangers conquer from the Israelites remains the possession of the Israelites. Some editors evidently thought that the graves of the ancestors might provide a better title. In Genesis xxiii Abraham buys a grave site[19] from the Hethites (Hittites). This is many generations before there is any suggestion of conquest by force. And even after David had conquered the Jebusites and taken Jerusalem by force we find that he purchases for cash an altar site which in due course becomes the site of the Temple itself (2 Samuel xxiv. 24; 2 Chronicles iii. 1). But according to the rules the *purchase* of land was not legitimate either. Leviticus xxv. 23–4 is quite unambiguous. Land may be transferred by mortgage sale but the ultimate title is unaffected: 'The land shall not be sold for ever: for the land is mine; for ye are strangers and sojourners with me. And in all the land of your possession ye shall grant a redemption of the land'.[20] But what is good for an Israelite must be good for a Canaanite or a Hittite or an Edomite as well. Why should not the Hittites 'ultimately' redeem the land which they sold to Abraham? This is an awkward question around which many Biblical stories seem to hinge.

The only fully legitimate mode of acquiring title to land is by inheritance (Exodus xxxii. 13). The rule of inheritance is embodied in the story of the daughters of Zelophehad (Numbers xxvii. 7–11). Land is ordinarily in the possession of men and is ordinarily inherited by the nearest male patrilineal kin but, in the absence of sons, a man's daughters will inherit before his brothers. It follows that, in ancient Judaea, title to land must often have been held by women. The rule of endogamy, which was probably more fiercely applied to women than to men (e.g., the story of Dinah above), thus had the effect of preventing land from passing out to strangers through the marriage of property-endowed women. On the other hand, by declining to marry with strange women Jewish males were prevented from gaining legitimate title to the land of strangers.

These legal details must constantly be borne in mind when considering the significance of the stories which follow.

If legitimacy of title depends exclusively on inheritance then genealogies assume paramount importance. What can we learn about the legitimacy of Solomon's title from a consideration of his genealogy?

In the Old Testament the genealogy of the House of David emerges only piecemeal but in the New Testament Matthew and Luke both trace the descent of Jesus Christ in a patrilineal line from Abraham through David down to St Joseph. Matthew's list of fourteen generations from Abraham to Solomon is consistent with the Old Testament record but is peculiar in that, in addition to the fourteen men, it names four of their wives, each of whom is a prominent Old Testament personality. St Matthew's Gospel is addressed to Jewish Christians and it can hardly be doubted that the genealogy as there cited is in a form which would be generally acceptable to Hellenized Jews of the late first century A.D. We must infer therefore that the four women in question have something in common which makes them specially significant as ancestresses of Solomon. Christian commentators offer no convincing explanation. The four are Tamar, Rachab, Ruth and Bath-Sheba. Let us examine their stories one by one:

I. TAMAR (Genesis xxxviii)

A. 1. Judah breaks the endogamy rule by taking a Canaanite woman, Shuah, as wife (Bath-Shuah in 1 Chronicles ii).

2. By her he has three sons, Er, Onan, Shelah.

3. Judah arranges the marriage of Er to Tamar.

– Tamar's ancestry is unspecified but, by implication, it is pure not foreign.

4. Judah's sin is punished by the death of Er.

5. Judah instructs Onan to fill the duties of a *levir* and raise up heirs to his dead brother's name. Onan refuses.

6. For this sin, Onan dies.

7. Judah promises Tamar that Shelah shall act as *levir* when he is grown up, but Judah fails to fulfil this obligation.

8. Tamar disguises herself as a harlot and seduces Judah.

9. Of this seduction are born the twins Pharez and Zarah.

10. Pharez is a patrilineal ancestor of Solomon.

*Outcome*

Tamar's deceit is treated as virtuous. Judah has 'pure-blooded' descendants through his pure-blooded daughter-in-law Tamar, whereas his own original sons were all of tainted blood through their mother Shuah. Appropriately when Shelah's descendants appear at 1 Chronicles iv. 21–3 they are palace craftsmen (potters and weavers) of servile status. Furthermore Shelah is the same as Shiloh, a place name. This Shiloh is represented as the principal cult centre for all Israel until the establishment of the kingdom when it is superseded by Solomon's temple at Jerusalem. Shiloh was located well to the north in the vicinity of Shechem and Samaria.

B. In 2 Samuel xiii we meet with another Tamar. She is the daughter of King David by a foreign wife and is seduced by her half-brother Amnon who is pure blooded. Tamar's full brother Absolom later kills Amnon.

It will be observed that in the Genesis story it is Onan the *half-blood* son of Judah who is killed because he refuses to cohabit with his widowed *full-blooded* sister-in-law Tamar; in the Samuel story it is Amnon the *full-blood* son of David (Judah) who is killed because he does cohabit with his virgin *half-blooded* half-sister Tamar. The outcome of the latter story moreover is the opposite to the first; none of the parties concerned have descendants and the succession passes to the line of Solomon, whose mother appropriately enough is called 'Daughter to Shuah' (see p. 61).

## II. RACHAB

Rachab the spouse of Salmon in St Matthew's list is traditionally identified as Rahab the harlot of Jericho whose adventures are recounted in Joshua ii and vi. Old Testament references do not name spouses for either Salmon or Rahab but the latter has always been treated as a Jewish saint. One Talmudic tradition makes her the wife of Joshua. Some quite orthodox textual critics recognize a possible link between this lady and Rechab, the presumptive ancestral founder of the

Rechabites, a puritan sect mentioned in Jeremiah xxxv and elsewhere. It is structurally appropriate that they should be identical. The Rechabites are tent dwellers and referred to as 'Kenites', i.e. descendants of Cain, through Jabal who was 'the father of such as dwell in tents' (1 Chronicles ii. 55; Genesis iv. 20). A tortuous trail through Exodus iii. 1; Genesis xxxv. 4; Judges i. 16 and iv. 11; Deuteronomy xxxiv. 3; Joshua vi. 25 then leads to the conclusion that 'the children of the Kenite Moses father-in-law' who joined forces with the children of Judah after the destruction of Jericho are identical with the father's household of Rahab the harlot 'who dwelleth in Israel even unto this day'.

The appearance of Rahab as an ancestress of Solomon thus brings to mind a whole string of binary discriminations. Jericho 'the city of palm trees' is a city of the plain which was utterly destroyed save only for the virtuous harlot Rahab who has virtuous descendants, Rechabite-Kenites. Sodom, another city of the plain, was utterly destroyed save only for the virtuous Lot who then engaged in drunken incest with his daughters from whom are descended sinful foreigners, Ammonites and Moabites. Rahab's ascetic descendants live in tents and not cities and are contrasted favourably with their sinful neighbours 'the men of Judah and the inhabitants of Jerusalem' (Jeremiah xxxv). For their virtue it is promised that their stock shall endure for ever; in contrast, city-dwelling Kenites are promised certain disaster (Numbers xxiv, 21). Lot's virtue in Sodom turns to sin afterwards and the sin is that of ignoring endogamy altogether.

It will be seen that these stories mix together the following antitheses: Israelite/Foreigner, Endogamy/Exogamy, Tent Dweller/City Dweller, Virtue/Sin. This is a pattern which has been present from the beginning. Genesis iv, 12–22 contrasts Cain (a vagabond wanderer, a fratricide sinner, a saint protected by God) with his son Enoch (the first builder of a city). From Enoch are descended three lines (i) the children of Jabal who are tent-dwelling pastoralists (ii) the children of Jubal who are musicians (iii) the children of Tubal-cain who are metal workers. Metal workers and travelling musicians would be almost the only categories of persons who would be equally welcome among nomadic Bedouin and settled agriculturalists. In structuralist jargon 'they mediate the opposition between Cain and Enoch'.[21]

*Outcome*

The implication of making Rahab the spouse of Salmon is that her harlotry, like that of Tamar, becomes a virtue. The adoption of her family into the Israelite congregation allows her child to be classed as legitimate, so Salmon has children who are classed as pure-blooded even though their mother is by birth a foreigner. Vowel signs apart, Hebrew Salmon is the same as Hebrew Solomon, so Rahab's virtue is the counterpart of the sin of Solomon's foreign wives.

## III. RUTH

That the story of Ruth is in some sense a 'parallel' of the story of Tamar is expressly recognized in the text (Ruth iv, 12). The Ruth story runs as follows:

1. Elimelech of the tribe of Judah is married to an Israelite woman of pure descent, Naomi.

2. By her he has two sons.

3. Elimelech dies. The two sons break the endogamy rule and marry Moabite women, Orpah and Ruth.

4. (The sin is punished by the death of the two sons.)

5. Naomi and Ruth return home to Bethlehem. Naomi advises her daughter-in-law to go after Boaz, a kinsman of Elimelech, so that the latter shall act as *levir*.

6. The arrangement that Boaz shall act as *levir* is eventually formally agreed according to the proper legal form before witnesses.

7. Ruth is made pregnant and bears a son Obed who is pointedly described as the *son of Naomi*, i.e. the child is a replacement of the two dead sons of Elimelech whose line is thus continued through the impure blood of Ruth.

*Outcome*

Ruth's behaviour is entirely virtuous, even though her original approach to Boaz is pointedly made to resemble that of a harlot (Ruth iii. 7–8). Elimelech ends up with descendants who are treated as pure-blooded even though in a genetic sense they are, like Salmon's children, part foreigner.

## IV. BATH-SHEBA

In 1 Chronicles iii. 5 this lady's name is given as Bath-Shuah, which makes her the namesake of the Canaanite wife of Judah. Her lineage status is ambiguous. A patched up genealogy makes her the granddaughter of Ahitophel the Gilonite, which would imply that she was of the tribe of Judah (2 Samuel xi. 3; xxiii. 34; Joshua xv. 51). But Bath-Sheba = 'daughter of Sheba' could imply that she came from Beersheba, a territory of the tribe of Simeon celebrated as being on the extreme southern frontier of Israelite territory. Sheba however is also the name of a Benjamite who leads an insurrection against King David (2 Samuel xx. 1). This Sheba took refuge, and was finally murdered at Beth-Maacah, a district on the extreme northern frontier of Israelite territory embracing Dan. It lies on the frontier of the land of Geshur. Absolom's mother, a daughter of the King of Geshur, is called Maacah.

These complexities serve to classify Bath-Sheba as 'a woman of Judah', a 'near foreigner' or 'a woman of Benjamin' according to choice; but they also offer an appropriate polarization of Bath-Sheba (Solomon) as 'a woman of the South (Judah)' against Maacah (Absolom) as 'a woman of the North (foreigner)'. Bath-Sheba was the wife of Uriah, the Hethite (Hittite), a foreigner serving in David's army. King David (Judah) lusts after her and seduces her: she conceives. David arranges that the virtuous Uriah shall be killed in battle; after which he takes Bath-Sheba to wife. The child is born but dies, as a punishment for David's sin. Bath-Sheba bears another son who is Solomon. Solomon is David's specified heir in preference to other older and more legitimate-seeming sons. These older sons had been born in Hebron and not in Jerusalem.

## Outcome

The son that dies was genetically David's but legally Uriah's. David's marriage to the widow ignores the levirate principle which has been emphasized in the Tamar and Ruth stories. Thus Solomon is very nearly, but not quite, 'a son of Heth' which would make him one of the original owners of Abraham's grave-site in Hebron. Note that if we accept the genealogy, David's ultimate alliance with Bath-Sheba is endogamous, she is of Judah, which makes Solomon a pure-blooded Jew. Contrast the original Judah's alliance with Bath-Sheba's namesake, who is explicitly a foreigner.

## V. ABIGAIL

A. The Bath-Sheba story is in certain respects the inverse of the Abigail story in 1 Samuel xxv:

David is not yet king. He encounters one Nabal a sheep owner of the house of Caleb. He seeks hospitality from Nabal which is refused. David plans to take revenge. Nabal's wife Abigail intercedes and David relents. Nabal dies ten days later, slain by God. David takes Abigail to wife. She has a son Chileab (Caleb) of whom nothing further is said.

*Outcome*

As in the Bath-Sheba story David's malevolence is responsible for the death of a husband of a beautiful woman whom David later takes to wife. Where Uriah is a 'good' man, Nabal is a 'bad' man. Uriah is a half-'outsider' – a Hethite fighting for David; Nabal is a half-'insider' – a Calebite of the tribe of Judah. Yet it is the child of Uriah's widow that is Solomon. It may be relevant that the claims of the 'sons of Heth' to Abraham's grave-site at Hebron are represented as antecedent to those of 'the sons of Caleb'.

B. The only other Biblical Abigail is also given as associate of King David. At 1 Chronicles ii. 16, Abigail and Zeruiah are sisters (or half-sisters) of David himself and their principal role is that they are respectively the mothers of Amasa and Joab, who are leading characters in a complex but highly structured story of feud and rebellion discussed below. Amasa's father is 'Jether (Jethro, Ithra) the Ishmaelite'. 2 Samuel xvii. 25, gives the father of Abigail and Zeruiah as Nahash[22] (i.e. the King of the Ammonites who had fought against both Saul and David (1 Samuel xi; 2 Samuel x). 'Jether the Ishmaelite' is reminiscent of 'Jethro the Midianite' another great keeper of sheep who was father-in-law to Moses (Exodus iii). Indirectly this links Nabal the husband of Abigail I with Jether the husband of Abigail II. If the two Abigails were merged into one person it would imply that

*either* (a) David marries his own half-sister, a very kingly act which puts him in the same class as Abraham and Pharaoh

*or* (b) David establishes by his marriage to Abigail a marriage alliance with the archtype foreign enemy, the King of the Ammonites.

This latter alternative would fit with 2 Samuel x. 2, since David would then be mourning for his father-in-law. If the two alternatives are combined the impossible compromise between endogamy and exogamy is perfectly achieved! The fact that Zeruiah and Abigail are daughters of Nahash (a foreigner) *and* sisters of David likewise compromises the endogamy/exogamy principles.

All told, it must, I think, be agreed that these five stories (Tamar, Rahab, Ruth, Bath-Sheba, Abigail) do keep harping in a single theme which centres around the question of whether it is possible for a 'pure-blooded' Israelite to beget legitimate children from a woman who is not an Israelite, or conversely whether it is possible for an Israelite woman to bear an Israelite child after cohabitation with a man who is not a pure Israelite. In a narrow sense the answer to both these questions is 'No', but legal fictions such as that embodied in the levirate rule or the principle that 'the child of a harlot has no father' permit the issue to become obscured.

If then we ask: 'Why should these equivocal ladies be mixed up with the genealogy of King Solomon?' the answer must surely be that, in terms of later Palestinian politics as distinct from Jewish sectarian religion, a doctrine of narrowly defined endogamous exclusiveness makes no sense. Moreover, taken all together, these stories make it possible to argue that not only is Solomon 'directly descended' from Jacob the Israelite, but that he is also 'directly descended' from Esau the Edomite and even from Heth the Canaanite, so that he is the legitimate heir to all forms of land title however derived!

Of course this is a quibble. But if Lévi-Strauss is right in his interpretations of myth, this is precisely the kind of quibble which a 'mythical history' is likely to contain. These same stories also illustrate another more general point, namely that, in mythology, 'sinfulness' is a very ambiguous quality which is close to 'godliness'. Cain the slayer of his brother became thereby a sanctified person protected by God,[23] and Biblical harlotry, though 'wrong', provides an easy road to sanctity through repentance. Tamar, Rahab, Ruth are all harlots after a fashion, but like Mary

Magdalene they are also all saints. The converse can also be true. A zeal for fulfilment of ritual obligations can sometimes turn back on itself and mark out the actor as a sinner. Saul's villainies when you come to examine them closely are strikingly similar to David's virtues.

So much for the strictly genealogical aspects of Solomon's justification but I have still not demonstrated the existence of structural order in any specifically chronological sequences of events as recorded in Biblical history. This I shall now attempt.

My procedure will be as follows: I take the Biblical text from 1 Samuel iv to 2 Kings ii and accept it at its face value, that is as a continuous history running from the death of Eli through the reigns of Saul and David to the succession of Solomon.[24] I provide an annotated precis, chapter by chapter, of the familiar story. Where my precis differs from the more usual type is that I pay attention to kinship status, and that I concentrate almost exclusively on the changing role positions of the principal *dramatis personae* and the relations between them. I assume as do structurally minded folklorists,[25] that there are really very few such 'principal roles' though, in the course of a sequence of stories, the same role may be filled by different individually named characters. Furthermore I start off with the basic assumption that the themes which we have already been discussing in this essay are likely to be constantly recurring, though that does not mean that these themes are the only ones which matter. In particular, I assume that the following antitheses, wherever they occur, have more than passing significance:

| Israelite | – Foreigner (e.g. Philistine, Amalekite, Ammonite, Geshurite, etc.) |

| | |
|---|---|
| House of Judah (as descendants of Leah) | – Houses of Joseph (Ephraim) and/or Benjamin (as descendants of Rachel) |
| Wives who are the daughters of Israelites | – Wives (and/or concubines) who are the daughters of foreigners |
| Fathers | – Sons |
| Full siblings (same father, same mother) | – Half-siblings (same father, different mother) |
| Legitimate king | – Usurper king |
| Priest (Levite) | – Non-priest |

While the main purpose of the precis is simply to give the order of events in which they occur, I also intersperse certain cross-references and commentary which are intended to draw attention to elements of 'structural' significance.

Let us then proceed:

## 1 Samuel

*Chapter* iv–vi The Ark is captured by the Philistines. Eli dies. The presence of the Ark causes disaster among the Philistines. [The True Faith and Foreigners cannot mix.]

vii The Ark is returned by the Philistines and placed at Kirjath-Jearim [which lies precisely on the border of the territory of Judah and Benjamin (Joshua xviii. 14). 2 Samuel vi. 2–3 refers to the same place twice over, first as 'Baale of Judah' and then as 'Gibeah' the Benjamite city of Saul.] Samuel acts as Judge over the children of Israel in Mispah. The Philistines are defeated.

viii Samuel's sons act as Judges but they are failures (sinners). The Israelites demand an hereditary king. [The stage is thus set for a battle over the kingship between Judah and Benjamin.]

ix–x Saul the Benjamite is selected by a process of randomized divination. Saul's destiny is shown by three omens, the first of which takes place at 'Rachel's sepulchre on the borders of Benjamin'. [At Genesis xxxv. 19, this place is described as 'in the way to Ephrath which is Bethlehem'. Bethlehem-Judah is the home town of the House of Jesse (cf. p. 52). He is finally chosen by lot at Mispah.

[There is a direct duplication and inversion between x. 11 and xix. 24. At the first reference, Saul's 'prophesying' indicates his regal potency; at the second it indicates his impotence and the regal potency of David.]

xi Nahash the Ammonite is defeated by Saul.

xii Prophet-judges are praised; kings are deplored.

xiii Saul is defeated by the Philistines but his son Jonathan is victorious.

xiv Saul threatens to kill Jonathan (xiv. 44) [because of a ritual offence].

xv Saul defeats the Amalekites but fails to kill Agag. Ritual slaughter of Agag by Samuel. God withdraws support from Saul and instructs Samuel to start again.

[At xiii. 9, Saul offends by sacrificing when he should not. At xiv. 24, Saul appears to be at fault for enforcing the ritual rules rather than for not doing so.

At xv. 22, Saul's specific fault is that he seeks to keep the ritual rules rather than listen to the instructions of God's prophet.]

xvi David is chosen. The selection is quite direct with no 'divination'. [Cf. xv. 23 which makes the surprising equation 'rebellion is as the sin of divination'. In fact it is David who rebels against Saul, but the contrast in selection procedures implies that it is Saul who is the rebel.]

David is now possessed by a 'good' spirit and Saul by an 'evil' spirit.

David becomes Saul's servant.

xvii David kills Goliath the Philistine.

xviii Jonathan loves David. Michal (Jonathan's sister) loves David and marries him. [From here through to xxiii *every* reference to Jonathan serves to emphasize his role identification with David. This equation implies that David ultimately replaces Jonathan as Saul's 'rightful' successor.

David's relation with Michal is much more ambiguous. His marriage to Michal connotes an *alliance* between the House of David and the House of Saul and this is quite a different principle of solidarity from that denoted by the *identification* of David and Jonathan. The specific 'alliance' aspect of the marriage is emphasized by the fact that David pays a brideprice to Saul of '200 foreskins of the Philistines'.]

xix Saul threatens to kill David [cf. xiv. 44 and xx]. Aided by Jonathan and Michal, David escapes. Saul's prophesying emphasizes his relative impotence [cf. x. 11].

xx David and Jonathan reaffirm their bond. Saul threatens to kill Jonathan [cf. xiv. 44 and xix].

xxi David is aided by the priest Ahimelech, who is betrayed by Doeg the Edomite.
David resides with Achish, King of Gath.
[This is the first of several incidents which serve to merge the antithesis Saul/David with the antithesis Saul/Foreigner, which is then (on the death of Saul) resolved as an antithesis David/Foreigner.]

xxii David rejected by Achish. David places his parents in the care of the King of Moab. He himself returns to Judah. Ahimelech the priest, betrayed by Doeg the Edomite, is killed by Saul's order. [This marks off Saul as irredeemably evil.]

xxiii David rescues a city of Judah (Keilah) from the Philistines. The people of Keilah betray David to Saul. David escapes to another city of Judah (Ziph). Jonathan reaffirms his solidarity with David. The people of Ziph betray David to Saul. David escapes. Saul fights with the Philistines. [The betrayal of David to Saul by his own people reaffirms the unity of the kingship despite the 'bad' cause of the King.]

xxiv Saul resumes his pursuit of David. David finds Saul asleep but does not take vengeance. Saul and David make peace. Saul recognizes David as future king. David promises not to wipe out Saul's family [cf. xxvi].

xxv Samuel dies. The story of David and Abigail (see p. 63).
David also marries Ahinoam of Jezreel [i.e. a woman of the House of Judah]. Michal, his wife from the House of Saul-Benjamin, is taken away from him and given elsewhere. [Judah and Benjamin are thus squarely ranged in opposition without any alliance between them.]

xxvi Virtually a repetition of xxiv with the difference that this time Abishai and Joab the 'sons of Zeruiah' (i.e. David's sister's sons) are mentioned as the champions on David's side and Abner (Saul's father's brother's son) as the champion on Saul's side. [As to the ambiguity of Zeruiah see p. 52.]

xxvii David, again in flight from Saul, again resides with Achish, King of Gath (see xxi). David pretends to Achish that he is his ally fighting against the Israelites, whereas actually he goes to fight against other foreigners, the Geshurites, the Gezrites and the Amalekites. His relation with these foreigners is itself ambiguous since we are later told that he marries the daughter of the King of Geshur who is the mother of Absolom and Tamar.

xxviii Saul at war with the Philistines consults the Witch of Endor. His doom is foretold.

xxix The Philistines go to war against Saul with David as their ally. The Philistines themselves reject the alliance, and

xxx David moves independently against the Amalekites and defeats them.

xxxi The Philistines move against Saul and defeat him. 'Saul and his sons' are killed. [This includes Jonathan but the text at this point does *not* mention the name of Jonathan.] The bones of Saul and his sons are buried at Jabesh Gilead. [The significance of this is connected with Judges xxi.]

## 2 Samuel

i David, still residing in Ziklag, a foreign town given to him by Achish (1 Samuel xxvii. 6), is told of Saul's death by an Amalekite who claims to have killed Saul. David executes the Amalekite [cf. iv]. He mourns for Saul.

ii David returns to Hebron in Judah and is made King of Judah. [Hebron is in the centre to the west of Jordan.] Abner installs Ishbosheth a son of Saul as King of Israel in Mahanaim [which is in Gilead to the east of Jordan].
The champions of both sides fight. Abner and the followers of Ishbosheth are defeated, but Asahel, a brother of Joab (David's champion), is reluctantly killed by Abner in an unorthodox manner.

iii Abner cohabits with Rizpah, a concubine of the deceased Saul [thus in effect usurping the throne of Ishbosheth (cf. xvi; 1 Kings ii)].
Abner now contracts a treaty of alliance with David.

Michal is restored to the status of David's wife [cf. 1 Samuel xxv].
Joab treacherously kills Abner, thus avenging Asahel.
David mourns for Abner.

iv Ishbosheth is treacherously assassinated by his own henchmen who are Beerothites (Beerothites are foreigners with the adopted status of Benjamites). David is told of this by the assassins and he has them executed [cf. i].

The more crucial of these events can be summarized as follows:

*As at 1 Samuel xxix*

Saul (Benjamin) is opposed to David (Judah).
Israelite is opposed to Foreigner.
David (Judah) is allied to Foreigner.

*Thereafter*

(i) Saul (Benjamin-Israel) is killed by a Foreigner who is killed by David (Judah-Israel). David mourns for Saul.

(ii) Abner (Benjamin-Israel) is killed by Joab (Judah-Israel) who is *not* killed by David (Judah-Israel). David mourns for Abner.

(iii) Ishbosheth (Benjamin-Israel) is killed by Foreigners-Benjamite-Israelites, who are killed by David (Judah-Israel).

*Outcome*

David (Judah-Israel) is sole survivor.
A very pure case of resolution through the mediation of opposites in the orthodox Lévi-Straussian manner. But let us proceed:

## 2 Samuel (continued)

v David made King of all Israel in Hebron. He captures Zion (Jerusalem) from the Jebusites (Foreigners).
He twice defeats the Philistines.

vi David brings the Ark from Kirjath Jearim to Jerusalem (see 1 Samuel vii).
David behaves as a prophet [cf. 1 Samuel x].
Michal disapproves and is condemned to childlessness.
[This seems to emphasize that the 'alliance' of the houses of

Saul and David is now irrelevant; from now on David's legitimacy is in his own right.]

vii David plans to build the temple in Jerusalem.
Nathan's prophecy assures the succession to the House of David.

viii David is victorious in further foreign wars. Foreign kings send tribute. [David is now established as an oriental despot of a unitary kingdom with a single sacred capital city.]

ix Mephibosheth, a surviving son of Jonathan who has been lame from infancy [and is therefore incapacitated from the kingship?] is given a status in David's household somewhere between that of a son and a servant [i.e. the same status that David originally had in Saul's household].

x Nahash the Ammonite dies (see 1 Samuel xi) and David offers mourning which is rejected. David's armies under Joab destroy the Ammonites and other foreigners.

xi–xii The story of Bath-Sheba and Uriah the Hittite (see pp. 61–2).
[In this position, this story amounts to a mediation of the Israelite/Foreigner antithesis.]

xiii Amnon, son of David and Ahinoam the Jezreelite, commits incest with his half-sister Tamar [cf. 1 Samuel xxv].
[For modern Christians, Amnon's sin is simply a grosser repetition of David's sexual offence of adultery. But in the actual text various kinds of offence are carefully discriminated. In the Bath-Sheba story we are explicitly told that Bath-Sheba was ritually clean when she cohabited with David and also that Uriah did not afterwards have sexual connection with his wife. David's offence is against the property rights of Uriah, it is not a 'sin' which entails ritual contamination. In sharp contrast, the real gravity of Amnon's offence is not that, as a royal prince, he cohabited with his royal sister, which borders on the legitimate, but that having cohabited, he then discards her, destroying her virginity without giving her the status of wife. The offence is one of ritual contamination. Absolom must avenge her not because his property rights have been infringed but because she has been dishonoured. Appropriately David's offence, which is a crime rather than a sin, ultimately results in the triumph of Solomon. Amnon's offence, which is a sin rather than a crime and the inverse of Onan's

offence of refusing to act as levir, ultimately results in the total destruction of all concerned. David's offence amounts to giving greater weight to the moral principle of endogamy than to the civil law concerning a husband's property rights over his wife. Amnon's offence is that he carried the moral principle of endogamy to excess, to a point at which 'correct' behaviour becomes sinful (cf. Saul's sin noted at I Samuel xv above).]

Absolom, full brother to Tamar and son of David by Maacah, a foreign princess (see p. 62) kills Amnon. [Note that Amnon is pure-blooded but Absolom and Tamar are half-blooded.]

David mourns Amnon.

Absolom takes refuge with his mother's father, the King of Geshur [cf. I Samuel xxvii].

xiv By Joab's intervention Absolom is brought home and forgiven [cf. xix].

xv Absolom leads an insurrection.
David takes flight supported by his bodyguard of foreigners. The priests remove the Ark from Jerusalem but David sends it back. [David is once again in 'foreigner' status as at I Samuel xxvii.]

xvi Mephibosheth (falsely) accused of treachery. Shimei, a Benjamite, calls for a renewal of the Judah-Benjamin feud. David declines to take offence.
Absolom asserts his kingship by sleeping with David's concubines [cf. iii; I Kings ii].

xvii The success of Absolom is attributed to his following the wise [i.e. Machiavellian] policies of Ahitophel the Gilonite. When Absolom changes his counsellor Ahitophel hangs himself. [By one reckoning Bath-Sheba is a granddaughter of Ahitophel (see p. 61). Observe that it is Absolom's failure to take Ahitophel's 'wise' advice which leads him to disaster. But later Adonijah's disaster results from his acceptance of Bath-Sheba's 'unwise' assistance (see 2 Kings ii).]
Amasa is made Absolom's champion. (Amasa is son of Abigail and mother's sister's son of Joab.)
David retreats to Mahanaim [cf. ii].

xviii There is a battle between the two armies.
Despite David's instructions to the contrary Joab kills Absolom. David mourns Absolom.

xix By Joab's persuasion King David is brought home to Jerusalem [cf. xiv].

Mephibosheth and Shimei are forgiven [cf. xvi]; but the Judah-Benjamin feud persists.

xx Sheba, a Benjamite, leads an insurrection.

Amasa (not Joab) is David's champion.

Joab treacherously kills Amasa. Sheba takes flight and is killed by his own supporters at Beth-Maacah (see p. 62).

Joab is again captain of David's army.

[Joab's killing of Amasa, his mother's sister's son, is 'close to' fratricide and comparable to Absolom's killing of Amnon at xiii.]

xxi (i) As a sin offering seven of 'Saul's sons' are, with David's consent, killed by the Gibeonites who are (like the Beerothites) foreigners with the adopted status of Israelites. The ambiguous text implies that five of the seven are sons born to Michal while she was separated from David.

(ii) David reburies the bones of Saul and Jonathan in their home sepulchre at Kish.

(iii) David's champions fight further successful battles against the Philistines. 'Jonathan the son of Shimei (Shimeah) the brother of David' kills a giant the son of Samson.

[In each of these three episodes the distinction between the House of Saul (Benjamin) and the House of David (Judah) is expressly repudiated. The blood-feud is paid off, the original blood-brotherhood of David and Jonathan is, by implication, reaffirmed.]

xxii Praise psalm.

xxiii A catalogue of David's glory.

xxiv David having transgressed the law, famine ensues. He purchases a site [for the temple] from the Jebusites (see pp. 47, 56).

## 1 Kings

i. David is old. He takes a virgin (Abishag) as concubine: she remains a virgin.

Adonijah, David's son, leads an insurrection, challenging Solomon for the succession. He is supported by Joab. Solomon is supported by Benaiah, a priest.

[Adonijah's mother is given as Haggith without further elaboration. A very plausible textual emendation makes this 'woman of Gath', balancing Absolom's mother who was a 'woman of Geshur'. On this basis Adonijah, like Absolom, was a half-blood.]

Solomon, son of David and Bath-Sheba, is appointed legitimate successor. Adonijah and Joab take flight but are forgiven. [It may be significant that they do not take flight abroad; they seek sanctuary in a temple.]

ii. David dies.

Adonijah, with the aid of Bath-Sheba, seeks to obtain David's concubine Abishag [cf. 2 Samuel iii. xvi].

Solomon treats this as an act of treason and Adonijah and Joab are both executed by Benaiah.

Solomon the King, Benaiah the priest-captain and Zadok the high priest rule in their glory.

Shimei, the Benjamite (2 Samuel xvi, xix) disobeys Solomon's orders by visiting Achish, King of Gath [cf. 1 Samuel xxvii] and is executed. [Note that Bath-Sheba has a vicarious association with each of the insurrections. Her grandfather Ahitophel is Absolom's counsellor (2 Samuel xvii), Sheba (xx) bears her patronym, she intercedes for Adonijah with fatal results (1 Kings ii). This 'marginality' of her political role is fully consistent with her other attributes (see pp. 61–2).]

I think that any reader who follows through the familiar story in the way I have presented it must recognize the existence of a pattern without perhaps being quite sure what the pattern is. The underlying structure becomes more obvious if we drastically reduce the number of *dramatis personae*, and think of the story as a three-phase unit in which the same characters keep appearing on stage in different costumes.

Table A summarizes the principal sexual and homicidal incidents roughly in the order in which they occur in the narrative, and specifies the more notable relational attributes of the individuals concerned.

Table B reduces the whole thing to a 'pattern'. The story then appears as a three act play.

## Act I

Prologue : David-Abigail-Nabal (Adultery) [1 Samuel xxv (inserted)].
Scene I : David and Saul (Judah v. Benjamin [1 Samuel iv–xxxi].
Scene II : David and Ishbosbeth (Judah v. Benjamin, + adultery with former King's concubine) [2 Samuel i–x].

## Act II

Prologue : (a) David-Bath-Sheba Uriah (Adultery) [2 Samuel xi–xii].
(b) Amnon-Tamar-Absolom (Half-sibling Incest) [2 Samuel xiii].
Scene I : Absolom and David (Son v. Father, + adultery with Father's concubine) [2 Samuel xiv–xix].
Scene II : Sheba and David (Benjamin v. Judah) [2 Samuel xx–xxiv].

## Act III

Prologue : David-Abishag (Impotence) [1 Kings i. 1–4].
Scene : Adonijah and Solomon (Half-brother v. Half-brother, + attempted adultery with former Father-King's concubine) [1 Kings i. 5–11. 46].

The 'play' develops two themes in parallel. The first is that of *sex relations*. The sections of the story which I have called 'prologues' ring the changes on sexual excess and sexual inadequacy. The second is a problem of *political relations*. In each 'scene' an anti-King (usurper) struggles for supremacy against a legitimate

TABLE A  *Principal characters approximately in order of their elimination*

| NAME | Relationship to David | Mother's Name | Mother's Lineage | Lineage of father (or stepfather) | Fate |
|---|---|---|---|---|---|
| Nabal | wife's husband | | | Judah (Caleb) | dies of David's malevolence |
| Abigail | wife/sister | | | ambiguous (see p. 63) | " " " " |
| Saul | wife's father | | | Benjamin | dies in battle, killed by Amalekite |
| Jonathan | wife's brother, adopted brother | | | Benjamin | " " " " , |
| Asahel | sister's son | Zeruiah | Foreigner (see p. 63) | unspecified | killed by Abner, reluctantly |
| Abner | wife's paternal uncle | | | Benjamin | murdered by Joab |
| Ishbosheth | wife's brother | | | Benjamin | murdered by his own followers |
| Michal | wife | | | Benjamin | dies childless (see pp. 70, 73) |
| Uriah | wife's husband | | | Canaanite (Heth) (see pp. 61-2) | dies of David's malevolence. Killed in battle |
| Bath-Sheba | wife | | | | survives |
| Amnon | son | Ahinoam | Judah (Jezreel) | Judah | murdered by Absolom |
| Tamar | daughter | Maacah | Foreigner | Judah | seduced and deserted by Amnon |
| Absolom | son | Maacah | Foreigner | Judah | killed in battle (near murder) by Joab |
| Amasa | sister's son | Abigail | (see p. 63) | unspecified | murdered by Joab |
| Sheba | none | | | Benjamin | murdered by his own followers |
| Shimei | none | | | Benjamin | executed by Solomon |
| Abishag | concubine | | Foreigner | unspecified | remains a virgin |
| Adonijah | son | Haggith | Foreigner (see p. 63) | Judah | executed by Solomon |
| Joab | sister's son | Zeruiah | | unspecified | executed by Solomon |
| Benaiah | none | | | Levite | survives. Solomon's champion |
| David | ..... | | (see pp. 61-2) | Judah | dies natural death |
| Solomon | son | Bath-Sheba | (see pp. 61-2) | Judah | survives as King |

# TABLE B  Overall Dramatic Structure

| DRAMATIS PERSONAE | ACT I | | | ACT II | | | | ACT III | |
|---|---|---|---|---|---|---|---|---|---|
| | *Prologue* | *Scene I* | *Scene II* | *Prologue* (a) | *Prologue* (b) | *Scene I* | *Scene II* | *Prologue* | *Scene* |
| Anti-King (Usurper) | David | David | David | David | Amnon | Absolom | Sheba | | Adonijah |
| Anti-King's Champion | | (Jonathan) | Asahel | | | Amasa | Shimei | | Joab |
| Female Intermediary | Abigail | Michal | Michal | Bath-Sheba | Tamar | | | Abishag | Bath-Sheba Abishag |
| King's Champion | | Jonathan | Abner | | | Joab | Amasa | Benaiah | |
| King (Legitimate right-holder) | Nabal | Saul | Ishbosheth | Uriah | Absolom | David | David | David | Solomon |

King. In each case anti-King and King are supported by champions. In the course of the story the opposition between rival lineages (Judah v. Benjamin) is replaced by a rivalry between father and son and then by a rivalry between half-brother and half-brother, a convergence which is paralleled on the sexual side by 'adultery with a rival's wife', 'adultery with a father's concubine' and 'incest with a half-sister'. David the original anti-King moves across the board to the position of King and the champions Amasa and Joab make corresponding moves in matching repetition.

The varying statuses of the women tie in both themes with the issue of endogamy/exogamy// Israelite/Foreigner. Each of the anti-Kings is tainted with Foreignness : David and Sheba both conduct their battles from frontier towns (Ziklag, Beth-Maacah); Absolom and Adonijah are half-bloods. But they are never classified outright as foreigners as are the Philistines, Amalekites, etc. The corresponding sexual puzzle implicit in the endogamy rule has already been discussed at length.

In 'Act III' the sexual and political themes are brought directly together in that the final bone of contention is *both* the Kingship *and* the sexual possession of Abishag. Notice here the role reversal of the meditator Bath-Sheba. At 1 Kings i. 17 she intercedes with David on behalf of Solomon *against* Adonijah, thus placing Adonijah in the status of usurper; at 1 Kings ii. 19 she intercedes with Solomon *on behalf* of Adonijah, and again puts Adonijah in the status of usurper. Destiny is destiny; all women are evil; the rebellious shall meet with their just deserts. When the rightful King (in the person of Solomon) is finally established his first acts are to wipe out (*a*) the surviving usurper (Adonijah), (*b*) the surviving champion of the House of David (Joab), (c) the surviving champion of the House of Saul (Shimei), thus bringing the story to a suitable 'clear stage' conclusion.

The view that 'history' in the Old Testament has more in common with drama than with history in an ordinary academic sense is not in itself at all new. This was indeed the favourite doctrine of the 'Myth and Ritual' school[26] and even the relatively orthodox von Rad points out that Saul's disasters seem to follow one upon another with the inevitability of Greek tragedy.[27] But it is one thing to sense the existence of a dramatic structure and another to show just what it is. I think that I have demonstrated the existence of a kind of patterning which was not previously suspected. Whether any particular reader considers this significant will be largely a matter of taste.

What then are the results of this exercise?

Firstly, the analysis shows that, in this case, the chronological sequence is itself of structural significance. This was not the case for most of the material examined earlier in this essay, where the variations-on-a-theme would be unaffected by the order in which they are cited.

Secondly, the analysis makes extended use of the genealogical and geographical detail which is so lavishly provided by the text. There are fashions in these matters. Modern theologians, Jewish and Christian alike, generally presume that these details have ceased to be relevant; nineteenth-century writers with their more reverent attitude to the infallible accuracy of 'gospel truth' felt it necessary to explain the genealogies away by postulating a folk memory of ancient tribal movements. But to the anthropologist the prolix details of 'who begat whom' seem all-important. He takes it for granted that details of past kinship and affinal connections are 'remembered' only as justification for the assertion of rights. If, in a field-work situation, the investigator is gratuitously informed that 'A was mother's brother to B' he should assume that this fact is socially significant. He should then consider 'Now just why should it be so important to remember that A was mother's brother to B?' And so also in the Biblical case. If the text informs us that X and Y were related in a certain way, then we should immediately assume that this information is of social significance, and needs to be related to everything else that the text may tell us about the mutual statuses of X and Y. If women are gratuitously added to a patrilineal genealogy the same argument applies.

The cases which I have analyzed provide substantial support for this assumption. In demonstrating this I am also demonstrating that the thought processes of the Biblical compilers differed from our own in this special way. This seems to me to be a point with wide implications for the understanding of ancient history.

Thirdly, and distinctively, this kind of analysis rests on a presumption that the whole of the text as we now have it *regardless of the varying historical origins of its component parts* may properly be treated as a unity. This contrasts very sharply with the method of orthodox scholarship. In the latter the occurrence of palpable duplication, inconsistency, etc., is treated as evidence of a corrupt text. The task of the scholar is then to sift the true from the false, to distinguish one ancient version from another ancient version and so on. For orthodox scholarship, the present text is not a unity but an amalgamation of documents which are still capable of being distinguished. I do not for a moment wish to challenge this proposition but I greatly wonder whether the effort can be worthwhile.

The unscrambling of omelettes is at best laborious and is not likely to improve the taste! If we treat the text as a unity then the ordinary distinction between myth and history disappears. The historical portions of the Old Testament constitute a unitary myth-history which functioned as a justification for the state of Jewish society at the time when this part of the Biblical text achieved approximate canonical stability. Scholarship cannot demonstrate precisely what this date was. It was earlier than A.D. 100 and probably later than 400 B.C. but it was certainly many centuries later than the purported date of the happenings which have been mentioned in this essay. So far as the mythical validity of these stories *at that date* is concerned the question of historical authenticity is irrelevant.

For ordinary men, as distinct from professional scholars, the significance of history lies in what is *believed* to have happened, not in what *actually* happened. And belief, by a process of selection, can fashion even the most incongruent stories into patterned (and therefore memorable) structures. For a contemporary English schoolboy, the really memorable facts about English sixteenth-century history are details such as the following:

*a*) Henry VIII was a very successful masculine King who married many wives and murdered several of them.
*b*) Edward VI was a very feeble masculine King who remained a virgin until his death.
*c*) Mary Queen of Scots was a very unsuccessful female King who married many husbands and murdered several of them.
*d*) Queen Elizabeth was a very successful female King who remained a virgin until her death.

*e*) Henry VIII enhanced his prestige by divorcing the King of Spain's daughter on the grounds that she had previously been married to his elder brother who had died a virgin.

*f*) Queen Elizabeth enhanced her prestige by going to war with Spain having previously declined to marry the King of Spain's son who had previously been married to her elder sister (Queen Mary of England).

It is not only in the pages of the Old Testament that the 'facts of history' come to be remembered as systems of patterned contradiction!

This bears on the larger issue of the relation between history and hermeneutic (and/or that between history and dialectic). Patterned structures in the surviving historical record (or in the *remembered* historical record) do not embody *intrinsic* moral implications. The patterning is simply a logical ordering of the parts, in itself it is morally neutral. But as soon as moral judgments are injected into any part of the system – as soon as it is postulated that 'A is a good man and B is a bad man' then, automatically, the logical ordering of the system causes the *whole* story to be permeated through and through with moral implication; the structure becomes 'dramatic'.

Furthermore, once an 'historical' text such as that of the Old Testament has become completely stabilized by a process of canonization the logical structure which it contains is also fixed. Thereafter, Jew and Christian and Moslem alike can use the same texts and derive different moral injunctions, even while relying on the same logical contrasts and mediations. The fact that the writers of sermons are unaware that this is how the process works does not alter the fact that this is what they do.

And I would add one final point about verifiability.

Those professional anthropologists who remain sceptical about the *bona fides* of the Lévi-Straussian technique are wont to complain that the materials which
Lévi-Strauss uses are so exotic and his principles of
evidence selection so arbitrary that all verification is
impossible. If only all the evidence were available
then the defects of the analysis would be palpable.
Well, in this Biblical case, all the evidence is very
readily available and different types of analytical procedure can be directly compared. Robert H. Pfeiffer is
a modern orthodox Biblical historian of the first rank,
and he analyses at length precisely the same story of
the succession of Solomon as I have done.[28] He uses a
simpler, more straightforward procedure and he finds
in the story nothing more exciting than a prosaic account of a sequence of actual historical events. This
procedure is essentially the same as that of Josephus
in *Antiquities of the Jews*, Books VI and VII. If literal-
ists prefer it that way, I am happy to leave it at that.

# VIRGIN BIRTH

## *The Henry Myers Lecture 1966*

There are three partners in every birth: God, father and mother.—Talmud, *Kiddush* 30 b.

The so-called primitive ignorance of paternity is nothing else but a very imperfect knowledge that intercourse is a necessary though not sufficient condition of the women being 'opened-up' as my Trobriand friends put it.—Malinowski in Ashley-Montagu (1937:31).


This lecture contains three themes which follow logically one upon another even though my presentation requires that they be slightly jumbled up. In the first place I review the classic anthropological controversy about whether certain primitive peoples, notably the Australian aborigines and the Trobrianders, were or were not 'ignorant of the facts of physiological paternity' when first encountered by early ethnographers. I conclude, as others have concluded, that they were not. Secondly, I take note of the fact that the anthropologist's belief in the ignorance of his primitive contemporaries shows an astonishing resilience in the face of adverse evidence and I consider why anthropologists should be pre-disposed to think in this way. Thirdly, I suggest that if we can once lay aside this prejudice about ignorance and primitiveness we are left with some important problems for investigation. Doctrines about the possibility of conception taking place without male insemination do not stem from innocence and ignorance: on the contrary they are consistent with theological argument of the greatest subtlety. If we put the so-called primitive beliefs alongside the sophisticated ones and treat the whole lot with equal philosophical respect we shall see that they constitute a set of variations around a common structural theme, the metaphysical topography of the relationship between gods and men. Limitations of time will prevent any elaboration of this latter theme.

The rules governing the Henry Myers Lectureship are couched in very flexible terms but I should perhaps make it clear that, despite my title, I am not offering a contribution to theological debate. Professor Clifford Geertz (1966 : 35) has recently denounced my attitude to religious matters as that of 'vulgar positivism'. This intended insult I take as a compliment. Positivism is the view that serious scientific inquiry should not search for ultimate causes deriving from some outside source but must confine itself to the study of relations existing between facts which are directly accessible to observation. In consequence of this limitation, positivists, whether vulgar or otherwise, usually show signs of knowing what they are talking about, whereas theologians, even when disguised as Professors of Anthropology, do not. The merit of this essay, if any, lies in its method.

I have been provoked into tackling the particular topic of Virgin Birth by the critical comments of another American, Professor Melford Spiro (1966 : 110–112). A summary of the issue between us will provide a useful starting-point.

One of the first detailed accounts of Australian aborigine attitudes to sex was W. E. Roth's description of the tribes of North Central Queensland (Roth 1903). He concluded that his informants were ignorant of any causal connection between copulation and pregnancy. He described the beliefs of the Tully River

Blacks on this subject in the following words: 'A woman begets children because (*a*) she has been sitting over the fire on which she has roasted a particular species of black bream, which must have been given to her by the prospective father, (*b*) she has purposely gone a-hunting and caught a certain kind of bullfrog, (*c*) some men may have told her to be in an interesting condition, or (*d*) she may dream of having the child put inside her' (p. 22 §81).

This is a calm factual report. Ten years later Frazer completely rephrased the above quotation so as to ridicule the childish ignorance of the natives concerned (Frazer 1914: 5: 102). In 1961 (Leach 1961) I used this example to illustrate the regrettable consequences of this habitual Frazerian practice. I also added the following comment: '[It is not] a legitimate inference [from this statement of Roth's] to assert that these Australian aborigines were ignorant of the connection between copulation and pregnancy. The modern interpretation of the rituals described would be that, in this society, the relationship between the woman's child and the clansmen of the woman's husband stems from public recognition of the bonds of marriage, rather than from the facts of cohabitation, which is a very normal state of affairs.' Professor Spiro seems surprised by this formulation. He says that he supposes it must be 'an extreme position', he declares himself to be personally persuaded that Roth's statement must mean that the aborigines in question were 'ignorant of physiological paternity', and he asks 'by what evidence or from what inference can it be concluded that ... the statements mean what Leach claims that they mean?' ... and so on.

Professor Spiro is not of course a positivist. He believes that explanation consists of postulating causes and ultimate origins for the facts under observation.

He cannot understand the thesis that insight comes simply from seeing how the facts fit together. I do not expect him to agree with my philosophy, but I am astounded by the naivety of his anthropology. He is apparently quite unaware that almost identical questions have been asked many times before and that a huge literature of commentary surrounds Roth's original ethnographical report.[1] This suggests to me that the time has come to take another look at this almost legendary controversy. I have not much to say that is new but evidently much that is old is now largely forgotten.

What is really at issue is the technique of anthropological comparison which depends in turn upon the kind of 'meaning' which we are prepared to attribute to ethnographical evidence.

When an ethnographer reports that 'members of the X tribe believe that ... ' he is giving a description of an orthodoxy, a dogma, something which is true of the culture as a whole. But Professor Spiro (and all the neo-Tylorians who think like him) desperately wants to believe that the evidence can tell us much more than that – that dogma and ritual must somehow correspond to the inner psychological attitudes of the actors concerned. We need only consider the customs of our own society to see that this is not so. For example, a high proportion of English girls go through the *rite de passage* of a Church of England marriage service. In the course of this the husband gives the girl a ring, her veil is removed, her flowers are thrown away, a priest lectures her on the importance of childbearing, and she has rice poured over her head – a set of performances roughly analogous to those reported by Roth of the Tully River Blacks. But all this tells me absolutely nothing about the inner psychological state of the lady in question; I

cannot infer from the ritual either what she feels or
what she knows. She may be an outright atheist.
Alternatively she may believe that a church marriage
is essential for the well-being of her future children.
Certainly her ignorance of the precise details of the
physiology of sex is likely to be quite as profound as
that of any Australian aborigine. On the other hand,
the English marriage ritual does tell the outside ob-
server a great deal about the formal social relations
which are being established between the various
parties concerned, and this is true of the Australian
case also.[2]

It would not be profitable to thrash over the details
of the Australian material again. I have given the
necessary references in a footnote. I will simply make
the following summary points in justification of my
position *vis-à-vis* Professor Spiro.

1. The 'vulgar positivist' interpretation which I
published in 1961 and to which Professor Spiro takes
astonished exception in 1966 was suggested by Frazer
himself in 1950 (Frazer 1905 reprinted 1910: 1: 167,
336; cf. 1910: 4: 126) and probably derives from
some still earlier source. Elaborations of the argument
have previously appeared in Malinowski (1913), Radcliffe-Brown (1931), Ashley-Montagu (1937) and elsewhere.[3]

2. There are two classically established reasons for
supposing that the Tully River Blacks were not
ignorant of the facts of physiological paternity in any
simple sense. These are

(*a*) that they freely admitted to Roth that the cause
of pregnancy in animals other than man is copulation,

(*b*) Hartland (1894–6; 1909–10) assembled a vast
collection of mythological tales from all over the
world which related to the magical conception of

ancestral heroes and hero deities.[4] Some of these stories resemble very closely indeed the account given to Roth by the Tully River Blacks of how *ordinary* human births occur. Hartland thought that such stories were survivals from a state of primeval ignorance. Almost everyone would now reject such an interpretation. But if the existence of European tales about ladies who became pregnant after eating magical fish is not now held to imply that Europeans are, or were, ignorant of the facts of physiological paternity, why should such stories have this implication in the case of the Tully River Blacks?

3. A third reason for rejecting the supposition of simple-minded ignorance is the judgment of the more recent ethnographers. Meggitt (1962) for example remarks that the answers which a Walbiri makes to questions about conception depend upon who is asked and in what circumstances. 'In ritual contexts, men speak of the action of the *guruwari* (spirit entities) as the significant factor; in secular contexts they nominate both the *guruwari* and sexual intercourse. The women, having few ritual attitudes, generally emphasize copulation' (Meggitt 1962: 273).

4. Outside Australia the only society for which 'ignorance of physiological paternity' is commonly thought to have been well established is that of the Trobriand Islands. Malinowski's original statements on this point were very dogmatic. He asserted that 'knowledge of impregnation, of the man's share in creating the new life in the mother's womb, is a fact of which the natives have not even the slightest glimpse.' But later on he became much more guarded. The 1932 version was: 'The Trobrianders do not suffer from a specific complaint *ignorantia paternitatis*. What we find among them is a complicated attitude towards the facts of maternity and paternity.

Into this attitude there enter certain elements of positive knowledge, certain gaps in embryological information. These cognitive ingredients again are overlaid by beliefs of an animistic nature, and influenced by the moral and legal principles of the community ...' (Malinowski 1932: 21). As much surely could be said of any people in the world?

We should also note that in his original account Malinowski stated that the Trobrianders, like the Tully River Blacks, recognized the significance of copulation in animals though not in men. Moreover, as a result of investigations carried out in 1951, Dr Powell has reached conclusions strikingly similar to those of Professor Meggitt for the Walbiri and these findings are supported by independent observations recorded in Austin (1934).[5] Despite the fame of Malinowski, the Trobriand Islands do *not* provide a supporting case illustrating the possibility of total ignorance of the facts of life.

Where does this get us to? Ignorance is a relative matter and obviously we are all ignorant in some degree, particularly about sex. But I think that anyone who reads through the Australian ethnographic evidence with a mind reasonably free from prejudice must agree, not only that the balance of evidence is *now* heavily on the side that the aborigines were not 'ignorant about the facts of paternity' in any simple sense, but that the balance of evidence has *always* been that way. That being so, the fact that a long line of distinguished anthropologists, which includes Frazer and Malinowski as well as Professor Spiro, have taken the opposite view is a very intriguing fact. Spiro's attitude is in fact typical. He is positively *eager* to believe that the aborigines were ignorant and he accepts their ignorance as a fact without investigating the evidence at all; at the same time he displays an extreme reluctance to believe that the products of aboriginal thought can be structured in a logical way. This, of course, is a very ancient tradition. In anthropological writing, ignorance is a term of abuse. To say that a native is *ignorant* amounts to saying that he is childish, stupid, superstitious. Ignorance is the opposite of logical rationality; it is the quality which distinguishes the savage from the anthropologist. When Professor Spiro writes that 'Religion persists because it has causes – it is caused by the expectation of satisfying desires' (Spiro 1966 : 177) he is simply rephrasing the old Frazerian argument that hope springs eternal even in a context of total illusion. It is the same argument as that which affirms that if men perform magical rites before the start of a fishing expedition it is *because* they are deluded into believing that fish can be influenced by words and actions at a distance and they go on believing this *because* they desire to catch fish. In other words religion and magic persist in a context of ignorance.

Now the interesting thing about this argument, as exploited by Frazer and also by the neo-Tylorians, is that it is applied only to *primitive* contexts. Frazer, who had such unbounded contempt for the ignorant savage magician, offered no objection to the nightly recital of Latin grace in Trinity College Hall. One cannot legitimately interpret the reading of grace as evidence that the parties concerned are either superstitious or devout; why then should we make different assumptions when 'ignorant natives' engage in 'meaningless ritual'? If an Australian aboriginal woman announces her pregnancy by bringing into camp a frog of a particular kind or by vomiting after taking food from her husband this is not evidence that she believes these actions to be the 'cause' of her pregnancy in a physical sense. They are signs not causes. Grace in a college hall 'says' that the meal is about to begin or that it has just ended; the actual word content is totally irrelevant. Similarly the ritual actions described by Roth serve to 'say something' about the social situation and the social condition of the parties involved, they do not express the sum of aboriginal knowledge.

I am here reminded of the fact that while the ordinances of the University of Cambridge indicate that young men obtain degrees because they sit examinations, they do not specify that any prior knowledge is required to achieve this desired end. Yet Cambridge undergraduates are not ignorant of the realities of the situation. The relationship between ritual and copulation in aboriginal theories about the causes of pregnancy appears to be of a strictly analogous kind.

But in any case, as I have said already, what seems to me interesting is not so much the ignorance of the aborigines as the naivety of the anthropologists. It seems evident that Western European scholars are strongly predisposed to believe that *other people* should believe in versions of the myth of the Virgin Birth. If *we* believe such things we are devout: if *others* do so they are idiots. It is into this aspect of that matter that I should now like to inquire.

Let me first state my personal bias. I find it highly improbable on common-sense grounds that genuine 'ignorance' of the basic facts of physiological paternity should anywhere be a cultural fact. It is true that since human gestation lasts nine months and the first evidence of pregnancy can only be experienced several weeks after the act of intercourse which caused it and since in any case intercourse is a necessary but not sufficient cause of pregnancy, it is by no means absurd to suppose that there might be human groups which are quite ignorant of the role of the male; but consider the probabilities.

Human beings, wherever we meet them, display an almost obsessional interest in matters of sex and kinship. Presumably this has always been the case. Human beings have existed on earth for a very long time, during which they have displayed collective problem-solving intelligence of an astoundingly high order. Ethnography admits that with a very few exceptions all cultural communities now existing are fully aware of the physiological connection between copulation and pregnancy. The exceptional groups, which are alleged to be ignorant of this connection, appear to be fully the equal of their more knowledgable neighbours in such matters as technical ingenuity, complexity of kinship organization and so on. Moreover, the allegedly 'ignorant' groups are not living in lonely isolation in some fabulous ethnographical Shangri La, they are groups which have close political and economic ties with other peoples who are not 'ignorant of physiological paternity'.

My inference from all this is one of scepticism. If certain groups, such as the Trobrianders, have persuaded their ethnographers that they were ignorant of the facts of life, then it is because that 'ignorance' was for these people a kind of dogma.[6] And if the ethnographer in question believed what he was told it was because such belief corresponded to his own private fantasy of the natural ignorance of childish savages.

We meet with alleged ignorance of physiological paternity among peoples whom ethnographers rate as very primitive. This 'ignorance' is deemed a mark of the 'primitiveness'. In contrast the miraculous birth of divine or semi-divine heroes is a characteristic of the mythology of the 'higher' civilizations. Dionysus, son of Zeus, is born of a mortal virgin, Semele, who later became immortalized through the intervention of her divine son; Jesus, son of God, is born of a mortal virgin, Mary, who ... ; such stories can be duplicated over and over again. They do not indicate ignorance.

The Frazer–Hartland generation of anthropologists tended to adopt two mutually inconsistent attitudes to such stories. On the one hand, since virgin birth is plainly a non-rational concept, the stories could not have been invented by sensible civilized people – they were survivals from an earlier primitive stage of society. On the other hand, it was implied that the theology of the 'higher religions' was not amenable to anthropological investigation at all. Only the Catholic Fathers associated with the journal *Anthropos* could consider the possibility that the religions of primitive peoples might have theological merit in their own right.

It is a striking fact that the five volumes which Hartland devoted to the discussion of Virgin Birth (Hartland 1894–6, 1909–10) contain scarcely a single reference to Christianity and the corresponding volumes of *The Golden Bough* (Frazer 1906), despite their cynical tone, make no attempt to fit the details of Christian theology into a cross-cultural schema which also includes 'primitive' materials.[7]

Now in its Christian context the myth of the Virgin Birth does *not* imply ignorance of the facts of physiological paternity. On the contrary, it serves to reinforce the dogma that the Virgin's child is the son of God. Furthermore, the Christian doctrine of the physical-spiritual paternity of God the Father does not preclude a belief in the sociological paternity of St Joseph. Medieval Christians thought of St Joseph as a cuckold ... 'Joseph was an old man, an old man was he' ... but the authors of the Gospels of St Matthew and St Luke combine their account of the

95

Virgin Birth with a pedigree which places Jesus in the direct line of patrilineal descent from David *through Joseph*. In other words, the kind of interpretation which I put on Roth's evidence and which Professor Spiro finds so novel and unacceptable has been orthodox among Christians for about 1,600 years. The myth like the rite, does not distinguish knowledge from ignorance. It establishes categories and affirms relationships.

Ethnographers of the late nineteenth and early twentieth centuries were predisposed to discover cases of ignorance of physiological paternity by their reading in the theoretical works of McLennan, Morgan *et al*. McLennan's fantasy of the beginning of civilization was of a society in which men mated promiscuously and the only kinship recognized was that through females. Common motherhood, he argued, is a fact very readily recognized whereas the recognition of paternity would require reflection and rational thought and would therefore be a much later development. The evolutionist doctrine that systems of matrilineal descent represent an 'earlier stage' in the evolution of human society than systems of patrilineal descent was tied in to this idea that matrilineal kinship is more obvious than patrilineal kinship. It was not argued that ignorance of physiological paternity must *now* prevail in all matrilineal systems, but only that it must have prevailed in the 'original' human societies and that these original societies would on that account have been matrilineal. This whole set of ideas predisposed ethnographers who were searching for 'very primitive' peoples to think they might discover matriliny and ignorance of physiological paternity in close conjunction. Moreover, even when the matriliny wasn't obvious, this particular type of ignorance could be taken as the ultimate mark of primitiveness, and would thus confirm the anthropologist in his hope that he had discovered a fossilized living specimen of primeval man – which is precisely what the ethnographers of Australian aborigines imagined they *had* discovered.

Evolutionism in its crude nineteenth-century form is no longer the fashion but versions of the evolutionist argument are constantly being revised. This ties in with the fact that the quest for the ultimate primitive who is *quite different* from civilized man appeals very strongly to certain anthropologists. My own prejudices go all the other way. The data of ethnography are interesting to me because they so often seem directly relevant to my own allegedly civilized experiences. It is not only the differences between Europeans and Trobrianders which interest me, it is their similarities. This of course is a Malinowskian precept, but let us try to put it into practice. Let us go back to the Christians.

In the Christian case a careful distinction is made between Jesus' legal status *as a man* and his essential nature *as a god*. As a man he is the legal son of Joseph the husband of Mary, and in this legal sense he belongs to the lineage of David. In contrast, his divine essence derives from the fact that the male component of his conception was 'the holy spirit' which entered Mary's body by an unnatural route. The details of this were at one time the subject of much learned speculation, the general consensus being that Mary was impregnated through the ear.

The distinction between legal status and substance appears also in the matrilineal Trobriand case in the reverse sense. A Trobriand child is of the same legal lineage as the holy spirit (the *baloma*) which magically enters the mother's body by an unnatural route at the moment of conception, but the child's human substance and appearance derives from the mother's husband.

However, when the child is divine rather than human there is another factor which comes in besides the split between *pater* and *genitor* and that between descent and filiation. In the theology of Christianity it is not sufficient that Jesus as mediator should be ambiguously both human and divine, Mary must *also* function as a mediator and must therefore have anomalous characteristics when considered as a human being. And what could there be that is more anomalous than a human being who is sinless and a mother who is a virgin?

This is a point of some subtlety. If we take the whole range of materials relating to what *we* consider to be supernatural births we find, at one extreme, cases of the Trobriand type, where virgin births yield normal children from normal mothers. Next, we get myths of magical pregnancy in which, say, an old woman long past the age of childbearing is finally granted a child – as with the biblical stories of the birth of Isaac or of John the Baptist. Here the implication is that while the child is predestined to be a hero, the mother will remain a normal human being. Finally, at the other extreme we meet with virgin mothers of the Christian type where *both* child *and* mother are thoroughly abnormal.[8]

Theologians delight in paradox of this kind and the trouble with early anthropological discussion of the topic was simply that the anthropologists could not bring themselves to believe that their primitive informants might be armed with the ingenious sophistication of a Jesuit priest. But can we go any further than that? Can we offer any general explanation as to why people should maintain a dogma which seems to reject the facts of physiological paternity, or is each case peculiar to itself?

Tylor, Frazer and the latter-day neo-Tylorians assume that statements of dogma start out as mistaken attempts to explain cause and effect in the world of nature. Dogma then persists because these mistaken ideas satisfy psychological desires. As a vulgar positivist I repudiate such speculation about causes which are inaccessible to observation or verification. It may seem surprising that men persist in expressing formal beliefs which are palpably untrue but you won't get anywhere by applying canons of rationality to principles of faith. All that the analyst can usually do is to observe the circumstances in which the untrue dogma is now affirmed and study the context of this affirmation in other ways. As with the recital of grace in College Hall we learn what the recital 'means' by studying the situation, not by studying the words.

Is there then anything which a dogma of Virgin Birth 'says' about the society in which it is affirmed? Well, let us consider first the simple logic of the matter. The Christian myth is compatible with a social system that is essentially patriarchal, in which it is taken for granted that the rulers are so vastly superior to the ruled that class difference almost ossifies into caste, a society in which the lords never marry into the lower classes, but in which they will graciously deign to take slave concubines and elevate their sons to the ranks of the elite. Such societies have in fact repeatedly emerged in Christendom, notably in Byzantium and eighteenth-century Brazil, both countries where the cult of the Virgin was exceptionally well developed. It would need a lot of careful research to discover whether this correlation is other than accidental but it does seem to be a striking feature of Catholic colonialism (which distinguishes it sharply from the Protestant variety) that the rulers, with their bias towards Mariolatry have tended to pull their half-caste sons into the ranks of the elite. In contrast, the Protestant colonists who generally speaking tend to reject the myth of the Virgin Birth have always pushed their bastards into the ranks below, insisting that the status of ruler-god is exclusive to the pure-blooded. God and Jesus fit well enough into the English Public School ethos; the Virgin-Mother has no place at all.

I fully realize that many people will find this sort of treatment of Christian ideology quite shocking and even more objectionable than Weber's celebrated tie-up between Protestantism and the rise of Capitalism, but I am quite serious. The British nineteenth-century evolutionist anthropologists were mostly Presbyterian Scots soaked in a study of the classics and sharing, as far as one can judge, most of the paternalistic imperialist values characteristic of the English ruling class of the period. Their theories reveal a fantasy world of masterly men who copulated indiscriminately with their slave wives who then bore children who recognized their mothers but not their fathers (McLennan 1865: ch. 8). This fantasy had some indirect resemblance to features of American chattel slavery, but it bears no resemblance whatever to the recorded behaviour of any known primitive society or of any known species of animal. It was justified simply by *a priori* reasoning. In the beginning men would have been unable to recognize a casual connection between coitus and parturition so that although men would dominate and satisfy their lusts by violence the only form of recognized kinship would be consanguinity through female links. The result was a theory appropriate to Protestant not Catholic imperialists.

McLennan's arguments were accepted by his friend Robertson-Smith who passed them on to Frazer who passed them on to a host of admiring ethnographic correspondents. The whole argument was recapitulated in quite explicit form by Hartland and swallowed hook, line and sinker by Malinowski. That was back in 1913 and, as we have seen already, Malinowski later modified his position very considerably. But he retained his high regard for aristocracy, and even at the end of his life he still thought of 'culture contact' as a kind of patronage extended by paternalistic colonial powers towards their more primitive subjects. The ignorance of the Trobrianders was a necessary element in their continuing primitiveness.

By 1932 Malinowski's theory of Trobriand ignorance had been partly abandoned but there was still the matter of Trobriand mythology. There was for example, 'The marvellous land of Kaytalugi ("satiated copulation") peopled exclusively by sexually rabid women. They are so brutally profligate that their excesses kill every man thrown by chance upon their shores, and even their own male children never attain maturity before they are sexually done to death. Yet these women are very prolific, producing many children, male and female' (Malinowski 1932: 156). Notice how closely this Trobriand version of the Land of the Amazons resembles the anthropologists' own fantasies. McLennan's imagination ran to rabid men raping promiscuously their servile females; the Trobrianders' fancy devised a world of rabid women raping promiscuously their servile males. McLennan's dream emerged from the context of a patriarchal ruling class which expressed horror at the thought of any marriage between an upper-class male and a lower-class female; the Trobriand version belongs to a society with virilocal matriliny, likewise class stratified, in which women are given as tribute to political leaders.

Professor Spiro will be wholly unimpressed. He will still ask: But how can you *prove* that these associations of facts are relevant? Well, quite frankly, I don't claim to prove anything at all. In my vulgar positivist fashion I just want to put the pieces of the jigsaw together. When the pieces fit, I am interested. I think this sort of thing tells us something about Trobrianders and also about factors which have influenced the devolpment of anthropological theory. But I agree that we learn no more about the Trobrianders' factual ignorance than we do about McLennan's.

But I still haven't fully explained what I am trying to say. Since the whole business of belief in virgin mothers and ignorance of paternity has been the subject of a vast literature, what can be the point of my just recapitulating odd snippets?

Well partly I am interested in the problem of method. We are dealing here with statements which we know to be untrue; how should we interpret ethnographical statements about palpable untruth? There are various kinds of answer which can be offered to such a question. If we are Tylorians, we accept statements of belief at their face value. We can then follow the footsteps of Frazer and Hartland and assemble huge archives of apparently similar untrue beliefs from all over the world. We then have to ask: Why do all these people believe in something which is untrue? And if you imagine that there must be a straightforward single answer to such a question I think your only way out is to say that these false beliefs rest on childish ignorance. This was the answer offered by the evolutionists and by the Malinowski of 1913 and, in modified form, by Professor Spiro in 1966.

If we are not Tylorians we can say what Powell's Trobriand informants said. There are different kinds of truth. Which is also what good Catholics say: 'We know that virgins do not conceive; but we also know that the Holy Mother of God was and ever shall be an immaculate Virgin.' This is the sort of answer offered by religious people and it is an answer which I can respect. But I do not think it is the sort of answer which should be offered by professional anthropologists in the course of their professional duties. We are social analysts not theologians. From an anthropological point of view non-rational theological propositions can only serve as data not as explanation. So we are pushed back to vulgar positivism. What sort of positivist analysis is appropriate to the sort of ethnographical data which I have been discussing?

The method which I advocate is the one which Lévi-Strauss calls 'structuralist'. Structuralism (in this sense) entails fitting the pieces together to form a pattern. The pieces in each pattern must come from a single context and we cannot accept the technique of Frazer's comparative method where snippets of evidence were drawn from here, there and everywhere. On the other hand we do not need to go the functionalist whole hog and describe *all* the evidence from every context. Our aim is still comparative; we want to distinguish the variety of forms in which a single ethnographical pattern can manifest itself and then examine the nature of these variations.

The following examples show the importance of seeing such patterns as a whole rather than as a summation of odd elements. Frazer devoted two whole volumes of *The Golden Bough* to discussing the theme of Virgin Motherhood in a general muddle of corn-spirits, fertility goddesses, dying gods and what-have-you. He felt certain from the start that the virgin mother goddess was a survival from a matrilineal stage of social evolution. When he met with contrary evidence, he either suppressed it or else invented quite imaginary forms of social organization to account for the discrepancy. At one point he twisted some remarks made by the Sicilian Greek Diodorus concerning the status of Egyptian women so as to demonstrate that the ancient Egyptians had a system of matrilineal descent in which men married their sisters and succession passed from a man to his own son in the dual status of sister's son and daughter's husband (Frazer 1914: 5 44n; 6: 213 sq.; cf. Diodorus 1: 27: 1–2). I regret to have to report that our President's justly celebrated essay on the structure of unilineal descent groups overlooked this interesting system (Fortes 1953).

Frazer however suppresses the same Greek author's remark that 'The Egyptians hold the father alone to be the author of generation and the mother only to provide a nest and nourishment for the foetus,' which is clearly an extreme patrilineal doctrine (Diodorus 1: 80: 3–4). So also, when Frazer comes to spread himself in a mildly salacious account of south Indian temple prostitution (Frazer 1914: 5: 63) he suppresses a large part of the evidence because it conflicts with his basic matrilineal proposition, and also with his theory that the temple prostitute is rated as a goddess incarnate (Frazer 1914: 5: 71). By rescuing Frazer's suppressed evidence from oblivion I can perhaps display the merits of a structuralist procedure.

The locale is south Kanara. As in neighbouring Kerala most of the ordinary castes are matrilineal. The Brahmans are patrilineal and consider this fact to be an index of their social superiority. The original account comes from Francis Buchanan writing in 1801 (Pinkerton 1808–14: 8: 749). He tells us that respectable married Brahman women when widowed or neglected by their husbands might become wives of the deity. The marriage rite consisted simply of eating some of the rice which had been offered to the deity. If the woman then chose to live in the temple she had the status of a sort of priestess and was fed and clothed at the temple's expense. She was free to have sexual relations with any Brahman but ordinarily became the permanent concubine of a person of high standing such as a government official. Her children belonged to a special respectable section (Stanika) of a special caste called Moylar. Women of non-Brahman caste could take up a similar profession but had to live outside the temple; their children also were Moylar but of an inferior grade. Within the general caste of Moylar there were a number of distinct endogamous sub-groups. Succession among all Moylar was from father to son, but each resulting patrilineage followed the caste custom of its matrilineal founding ancestress. The ordinary Brahmans, while professing to despise the Moylar, in fact behaved towards them as if they had high ritual status.

In this case the mother is a widow, the legal wife of a god. She is made pregnant by the action of a human being. The son is the founder of a patrilineal descent line originating in his mother but having status qualities derived from the mother's divine husband. Although the mother and the physiological father may both be Brahmans, the son is not legally related to either of them since he is of separate caste. This last detail creates complications and the theory that the Moylar son should rate higher than the Brahman father is disputed.

Taken together these facts add up to a pattern of some complexity. But notice how the Christian data form a very similar pattern with all the elements reversed. In the Christian case the mother is a Virgin not a widow. She is the legal wife of a human being, not of a god. The Son is the last not the first member of his patrilineal line. Although the mother and the legal father are both human beings the Son is substantially related to neither of them since he is a god. This last detail creates complications and the theory that the mother is a lower order of being than the Son is disputed.

But we face the same kind of question as before. What is the point of arranging the facts in this way? How do I *know* that such patterns are significant? I don't. I find them interesting. If we go back to the Australian and Trobriand cases the data do not add up to the same identical pattern but some of the same variables recur.

In Australia the impregnating spirit child, like the Holy Ghost, originates in God (the Rainbow Serpent). In Australia the marriage ritual entails the woman accepting a gift of food from her human husband; in south India the woman eats food from the shrine of her divine husband. In Australia the ideology of filiation resembles that of Christianity. It is God (in the form of the Rainbow Serpent and/or the Totemic Ancestor) who is the recognized *genitor* of the child while it is the human husband (who alone has sexual access to the woman) who is the *pater* – a paradoxical reversal of the ordinary *pater-genitor* distinction. In the Trobriand case the impregnating spirit children come from Tuma, the other world. They originate as deceased ancestors of the mother's sub-clan. In sharp contrast to all the other cases discussed the mother and her child are here intrinsically related – they are of the same sub-clan throughout eternity. There is no deity who is 'other than' the mother, and the woman's husband has no status *vis-à-vis* the son either as recognized *genitor* or recognized *pater*. But the husband provides the physical substance of the child, and it is the husband who alone has sexual access to the woman.

If we studied other examples of Virgin Birth we should meet with the same variables in new combinations. We should also meet with new variables. For example, in the Attis/Adonis mythology discussed by Frazer there is a major reversal. The god is female and the recognized *genitor* a human being, but many of the other elements are similar to the Indian and Christian cases. I cannot here pursue these ramifications nor discuss in detail where they may lead to. I would merely remark that themes of descent, filiation and sexual and/or marital alliance between gods and humans necessarily have basic relevance for the symbolization of time and for our topographical apprehension of the other world.

Let me try to pull the various threads of my argument together. The crux is this. From many sources we learn of legends, traditions, ritual practices which seem to imply a belief that women may sometimes be made pregnant by means other than insemination by a human male. The simplest way of 'explaining' such a belief is to say that it is due to the ignorance of the believer. Many anthropologists have argued this way and some are still inclined to do so. They seem to gain reassurance from supposing that the people they study have the simple-minded ignorance of small children. That Frazer should have thought that way is understandable, that my contemporaries should do so is extraordinary.

An alternative way of explaining a belief which is factually untrue is to say that it is a species of religious dogma; the truth which it expresses does not relate to the ordinary matter-of-fact world of everyday things

but to metaphysics. It is plain, for example, that
Christians who say that they 'believe' in the doctrine
of the Virgin Birth or in the closely related doctrine of
the Immaculate Conception are not ordinarily argu-
ing from a position of ignorance; on the contrary these
are doctrines which are compatible with positions of
extreme philosophical sophistication. This type of
explanation is to be preferred to the other. Frazer's
childish savage should be eliminated from anthropological discussion once and for all; in his place we
should put a slightly muddle-headed theologian no
less ingenious than the Bishop of Woolwich or even
the cleverest of my anthropological colleagues.

The problem with which this muddle-headed theologian is concerned lies at the core of speculative
philosophy. What is the difference between the
physical and the metaphysical? One way of viewing
the matter is to equate the not-now with the other
world; in that case past and future coalesce as attributes of the other in contrast to the present which is
the factual experience of real life. The relationship
between the 'here-now' and the 'other' can then be
seen as one of *descent*. My ancestors belong to the
'other' category and so do my descendants. Only *I*
am in the here and the now. Of course, there is much
more than that to the matter of alternating generations and to the tendency to put grandparents and
grandchildren into one kinship category. All I am saying is that social distance in time and space and generation is very frequently and very readily dovetailed
in with a distinction between the living and the dead,
and this is relevant for an understanding of the
materials we have been discussing.

The relationship between the here-now and the
other can also be represented in other ways, for
example as one of class status and power – the gods

are perfect and powerful, men are imperfect and impotent; or as one of normality and abnormality – hence the supernatural birth and immortality of divine beings.

But the disjunction of the two worlds is not enough, there must also be continuity and mediation. Cross-cutting the idea that impotent men are the descendants of potent gods we have the incestuous dogma that gods and men may establish sexual connection. Dogmas of virgin birth and of the irrelevance of human male sexuality appear as by-products of such a theology; I do not claim that they are thus *caused*, but this is where they fit in, and this is the case in primitive as well as in sophisticated societies.

This lecture has necessarily been very incomplete but the main points which I would like to put across are these:

1. Anthropological theories often tell us more about the anthropologists than about their subject matter.

2. Let us remain sceptical and positivist. Try to see connections between the facts as we know them. Don't inject magical causal explanations from outside.

3. It is time that we finally abandoned the traditional distinction between the stupidity of savages and the theology of civilized men. Stories about ignorance of paternity among primitive peoples are of the same kind as stories about the virgin birth of deities in the so-called higher religions. And in neither case are the story-tellers stupid. If we are to understand such stories we need to consider them all together as variations on a single structural theme.

4. If anthropologists are to justify their claim to be students of comparative religion, they need to be less polite. So far they have shown an extraordinary

squeamishness about the analysis of Christianity and Judaism, religions in which they themselves or their close friends are deeply involved. Roth's Bulletin No. 5 on the North Queensland Aborigines was an ethnographic document of considerable interest; so is chapter i of the Gospel according to St Matthew. Serious anthropologists should treat the two works on a par; both are records of theological doctrine.

## REFERENCES

ASHLEY-MONTAGU, M. F., 1937. *Coming into being among the Australian aborigines* (London, Routledge).

AUSTIN, L., 1934. 'Procreation among the Trobriand Islanders', *Oceania* 5, 102–18.

FORTUNE, R. F., 1932. *Sorcerers of Dobu* (London, Routledge).

DIODORUS, see Oldfather, C. H., *Diodorus of Sicily*. English translation (10 vols.) Loeb Classical Library. (1932, vol. 1: 84–7, 274–5) (London, Heinemann).

FORTES, M., 1953. 'The structure of unilineal descent groups', *Am. Anthrop.* 55, 17–41.

FRAZER, J. G., 1905. 'The beginnings of religion and totemism among the Australian aborigines', *Fortnightly Rev.* n.s. 78, 162–72, 452–66.

FRAZER, J. G., 1906. *Adonis, Attis, Osiris.* 2 vols. in 1 (later vol. 5 and 6 of Frazer 1914) (London, Macmillan).

FRAZER, J. G., 1909. 'Beliefs and customs of the Australian aborigines', *Man* 9, 145–7.

FRAZER, J. G., 1910. *Totemism and exogamy.* 4 vols (London, Macmillan).

FRAZER, J. G., 1914. *The Golden Bough.* 3rd edn. 12 vols (London, Macmillan).

GEERTZ, C., 1966. 'Religion as a cultural system', *Anthropological approaches to the study of religion* (ed.) M. Banton (Monogr. Ass. social Anthrop. 3) (London, Tavistock Publications).

HARTLAND, E. S., 1894–6. *The Legend of Perseus.* 3 vols (London, David Nutt).

HARTLAND, E. S., 1909–10. *Primitive paternity.* 2 vols (London, Folk Lore Society).

ISHIDA, E., 1964. 'Mother-Son deities', *Hist. Rel.* 4, 30–68.

KABERRY, P. M., 1936. 'Spirit children and spirit centres of the North Kimberley Division, West Australia', *Oceania*, 6, 392–400.

KABERRY, P. M., 1939. *Aboriginal woman* (London, Routledge).

LEACH, E. R., 1961. 'Golden bough or golden twig?', *Daedalus*, Spring 1961 : 371–87.

MALINOWSKI, B., 1913. *The family among the Australian aborigines* (London, London University Press).

MALINOWSKI, B., 1932. *The sexual life of savages in north western Melanesia.* 3rd edition with special foreword (London, Routledge).

McLENNAN, J. F., 1865. *Primitive marriage* (London, Quaritch).

MEGGITT, M. J., 1962. *Desert people* (Sydney, Angus & Robertson).

PINKERTON, J., 1808–14. *A general collection of the best and most interesting voyages & travels in all parts of the world.* 17 vols (London, Longman, Hurst, Rees & Orme).

POWELL, H. A., 1956. *An analysis of present day social structure in the Trobriands* (Thesis, London).

PURCELL, B. H., 1893. 'Rites and customs of Australian aborigines', *Z. Ethnol.* 25, 286–9.

RADCLIFFE-BROWN, A. R., 1931. 'The social organisation of Australian tribes', *Oceania Monogr.* 1 (Melbourne, Macmillan).

ROHEIM, G., 1932. 'Psycho-analysis of primitive cultural types', *Intern. J. Psycho-Anal.* 13, 1–224.

ROTH, W. E., 1903. *Superstition, magic and medicine,* N. Queensl. Ethnogr. Bull. 5 (Brisbane, Vaughan).

SCHMIDT, W., 1952. 'Der Konzeptionsglaube australischer Stämme', *Intern. Arch. Ethnogr.* 46, 36–81.

SPENCER, B. & GILLEN, F. J., 1899. *The native tribes of Central Australia* (London, Macmillan).

SPIRO, M. E., 1966. Religion : problems of definition and explanation, *Anthropological approaches to the study of religion* (ed.) M. Banton (Monogr. Ass. social. Anthrop. 3) (London, Tavistock Publications).

STANNER, W. E. H., 1933. 'The Daly River tribes: the theory of sex', *Oceania* 4, 26–8.

STREHLOW, C., 1907–21. *Die Aranda und Loritja Stämme in Zentral-Australien* (Frankfurt, Baer).

TALMUD, *Kiddush* 30. b. *See* Epstein I, *The Babylonian Talmud: Seder Nashi VIII Kiddushin,* 1936, p. 149, translated H. Freedman (London, Soncino Press).

THOMPSON, D. F., 1933. 'The hero cult, initiation and totemism on Cape York: the knowledge of physical paternity', *J. R. anthrop. Inst.* 63, 505–10.
WARNER, W. L., 1937. *A black civilisation* (New York, Harper).

# NOTES

## GENESIS AS MYTH

1 J. Schniewind in H. W. Bartsch, 'Kerygma and Myth: a Theological Debate' (London, S.P.C.K., 1953), p. 47.

2 C. Shannon and W. Weaver, 'The Mathematical Theory of Communication' (Urbana, University of Illinois Press, 1949).

3 R. Jakobson and M. Halle, 'Fundamentals of Language' (The Hague, Mouton, 1956).

4 C. Lévi-Strauss, 'The Structural Study of Myth', *Myth: a Symposium*, ed. T. A. Sebeok (Bloomington, University of Indiana Press, 1955).

5 G. Groddeck, 'The World of Man' (London, C. W. Daniel, 1934).

See also E. R. Leach, 'Lévi-Strauss in the Garden of Eden', *Transactions of the New York Academy of Sciences*, 23, 4 (New York, 1961), pp. 386–96.

## THE LEGITIMACY OF SOLOMON

1 C. Lévi-Strauss, *Anthropologie structurale* (Paris, Plon, 1958), p. 81.

2 C. Lévi-Strauss, *La pensée sauvage* (Paris, Plon, 1962).

3 C. Lévi-Strauss, *Mythologivues: Le cru et le cuit* (Paris, Plon, 1964), p. 346.

4 C. Lévi-Strauss, *La pensée sauvage*, p. 173.

5 G. Ryle, *The Concept of Mind* (London, Hutchinson, 1949), pp. 15 ff. 'The dogma of the Ghost in the Machine' is Professor Ryle's label for what he calls 'the Official Doctrine', deriving from Descartes, which treats mind and body as separate entities. Ryle's book is designed to demonstrate that this dogma 'is entirely false'.

6 Morris Ginsberg (*On the Diversity of Morals*, London, Heinemann, 1956, p. 239) has translated a passage from Durkheim's *Sociologie et philosophie* (Paris, Presses univ. de France, 1924). pp. 74–5, as follows: 'Kant postulates God because without this hypothesis morality would be unin-

telligible. I postulate a personality, specifically distinct from individuals, because otherwise morality would have no object and duty, no point of attachment.'

D. F. Pocock in his translation of *Sociology and Philosophy* (London, Cohen and West, 1953), pp. 51-2, substitutes for the word 'personality' the word 'society', thus quite altering the degree of reification implied.

7 These comments are a free interpretation of part of what is argued at length by Paul Ricœur in 'Structure et herméneutique' in *Esprit*, November 1963, pp. 596-628. Ricœur makes extensive references to Gerhard Von Rad, *Theologie des Altes Testaments* Bd. I, *Die Theologie der geschichtlichen Überlieferungen Israels* (Munich, Chr. Kaiser Verlag, 1957), which has been translated into English as *Old Testament Theology*, vol. I, *The Theology of Israel's Historical Tradition* (London, Oliver and Boyd, 1962). Von Rad, like all orthodox Biblical scholars, takes it for granted that a fundamental core of 'real history' underlies the narrative at least from the time of David onwards. My own scepticism is far more radical: King David and King Solomon are no more likely to be historical than are King Agamemnon and King Menelaus.

On the other hand, I share M. I. Finley's view (e.g. 'Myth, Memory and History', *History and Theory*, IV [1965], pp. 281-302) that the distinction between myth and history is not necessarily clear cut. It need not be inconsistent to affirm that an historical record has mythical characteristics and functions. In point of fact Von Rad's historical assumptions, when modified by his refined techniques of textual criticism, often lead to conclusions which are entirely in accord with the implications of the 'structuralist' procedures exemplified in this essay.

8 E. R. Leach, 'Lévi-Strauss in the Garden of Eden', *Transactions of the New York Academy of Sciences* (1961), 23-4, pp. 386-96. E. R. Leach, 'Genesis as Myth', *Discovery*, XXIII (1962), pp. 30-5. Also pp. 7-23 of this book.

Lévi-Strauss seems to regard ethnology and history as complementary but quite distinct forms of inquiry [*La pensée sauvage* (Paris, Plon. 1958), p. 39]. This may explain why he uses a narrow definition of myth which makes it appear that the myths of contemporary Amerindians are cultural products of an entirely different kind from the mythical-historical traditions of the Jewish people in the first century B.C. My own view is that this distinction is quite artificial and that the structural analysis of myth should be equally applicable to both the time of men and the time of gods. (Cf. Finley, op. cit. p. 288.)

9 Apart from the sources mentioned in the text, the commentaries which I have found most useful are:

James Hastings, *A Dictionary of the Bible*, 5 vols (New York, T. and T. Clark, 1898–1904).

T. K. Cheyne and J. S. Black, *Encyclopaedia Biblica*, 4 vols (London, A. & C. Black, 1899–1903).

James Strong, *The Exhaustive Concordance of the Bible* (London, Hodder and Stoughton, 1894).

S. R. Driver and others, *The International Critical Commentary* (London, T. and T. Clark, 1895–1951).

Two useful bibliographic sources of a different kind are: G. Widengren 'Early Hebrew Myths and their Interpretation' in S. H. Hooke, *Myth, Ritual and Kingship* (Oxford, Clarendon Press, 1958), pp. 147–203.

R. Graves and R. Patai, *Hebrew Myths: The Book of Genesis* (London, Cassell, 1964).

10 For a recent full examination of the evidence see Aage Bentzen, *Introduction to the Old Testament*, 4th Edition (Copenhagen, G. and C. Gad, 1958). It is probable that a substantially orthodox text had been established by 400 B.C. but modifications were still being introduced in the first century A.D. and there was more than one canonical orthodoxy.

11 Graves and Patai (op. cit., 1964, p. 25) take note of the antiquity of this style of analysis. They are plainly scornful: 'This scheme and others like it, prove the Rabbis' desire to credit God with systematic thought.' As my citation from Leo Strauss shows, there is more to it than that.

12 Leo Strauss, 'Interpretation of Genesis' (typescript of a lecture delivered at University College, University of Chicago, January 25th, 1957).

13 If Nehemiah was a flesh-and-blood historical character then he lived about 400 B.C.

14 S. A. Cook, Article 'Jews', *Encyclopedia Britannica*, 14th edition.

15 From the point of view of general communication theory, randomly distributed minor textual inconsistencies may be looked upon as *Gaussian noise*. For a non-technical explanation of this point see C. Cherry *On Human Communication* (Cambridge, Mass., M.I.T. Press and John Wiley and Sons Inc., 1957), p. 198.

16 E.g. Evans-Pritchard, *The Nuer* (Oxford, Clarendon

# NOTES

Press, 1940). E. Peters, 'The Proliferation of Segments in the Lineage of the Bedouin of Cyrenaica', *Journal of the Royal Anthropological Institute*, XC (1960), pp. 23–53. M. Fortes, *The Dynamics of Clanship among the Tallensi* (London, Oxford University Press, 1946).

17 It deserves note that the fully historical Kingdom of Judaea of Simon Maccabaeus (second century B.C.) consisted of territory which, in the traditional narrative, was allocated to Judah, Benjamin and Ephraim. Samaria was at that time a separate province to the north. Ahab, the prototype 'bad' northern king in the traditional history, is specifically described as King of Samaria (1 Kings xvi. 29–30, xxi. 1).

In the genealogy, the tribe of Benjamin is linked with the tribes of Ephraim and Manasseh in that all are descended from Rachel, but Ephraim and Manasseh are the descendants of Joseph who becomes a foreigner. Joseph is the first of Jacob-Israel's sons to become separated from his father and the land of Israel. He becomes ruler of Egypt and marries an Egyptian. In contrast, Benjamin is the last of Jacob-Israel's sons to become separated from his father and his homeland (Genesis xliii, xlvii. 20).

18 In Hebrew as in English the phonemic difference between Zeruah and Zeruiah is slight, indeed in the lexicon of Biblical Hebrew the two words appear as adjacent entries. Some ancient texts imply that Zeruah was a harlot, but in Biblical contexts this too has ambiguous implications (see p. 64).

19 There is a flat contradiction between Genesis xxiii and l. 13 on the one hand, and Genesis xxxiii. 18–20 and Acts vii. 16 on the other. The first reference makes Abraham purchase a grave-site from the Hethites (Hittites) at Hebron; the second reference makes Abraham purchase a grave-site from the Shechemites at Shechem. David was first crowned king at Hebron; the secessionist Jeroboam was crowned king at Shechem. This contradiction, like the Calebite inconsistencies, must be a residue of editorial attempt to justify simultaneously two rival claims to the same title of ancestral right. As will be seen from the map, Hebron and Shechem are symmetrically located north and south of the east-west frontier.

20 In the story of Naboth's vineyard Naboth's virtue lies in the fact that he denies the right of King Ahab to buy out his inheritance with money (1 Kings xxi. 2–3).

21 Cf. Von Rad, op. cit., p. 64, also G. von Rad, *Genesis* (London, S.C.M. Press, 1961), p. 107.

22 Orthodox scholarship here presumes a corrupt text and would substitute 'Jesse' for 'Nahash'.

23 Cf. I. Schapera, 'The Sin of Cain', *Journal of the Royal Anthropological Institute*, LXXXV (1955). Part I, Jan.–Dec., pp. 33–43, discusses sociological explanations of the fact that blood revenge cannot be taken against a fratricide.

24 Modern Biblical scholarship recognizes this material as having a distinct and unitary core referred to by Von Rad and others as 'The Succession Document'.

25 Cf. V. Propp, *The Morphology of the Folktale* (Bloomington, Indiana University Research Centre in Anthropology and Linguistics, 1958).

26 Cf. Hooke, op. cit.; also Lord Raglan, *The Hero* (London, Methuen, 1936).

27 Von Rad, *Theologie des Altes Testaments*, p. 325.

28 Robert H. Pfeiffer, *Introduction to the Old Testament* (London, A. and C. Black, 1952), pp. 342–59.


## VIRGIN BIRTH

1 The literature on this topic is very large. Relevant source material down to 1936 is quoted in Ashley-Montagu (1937: 349–55). The details of the controversy as it developed from 1894 onwards are laid out in chapters 1 and 10 of the same work. The two basic standpoints remained unchanged throughout: Hartland and his followers held that on logical grounds there must have been a time when primitive man did not recognize the connection between copulation and pregnancy; Australian aborigines are in this respect examples of primeval man surviving into modern times. The other group which included Andrew Lang, Westermarck, Pater Schmidt and Goldenweiser denied that the actual evidence suggested that the Australian aborigines were ignorant in the sense suggested. The general consensus of anthropological opinion in the period before 1914 agreed with Hartland. The adherents of Hartland's opinion included Frazer and Malinowski (1913). The last-named however was already concerned to show that an ideology of ignorance could have sociological significance. Schmidt (1952) seems to be the only general review of the subject which is later than Ashley-Montagu (1937). Schmidt criticizes Ashley-Montagu's conclusions but does not cite any additional material.

Those who accepted Hartland's position relied principally

on evidence provided by Spencer & Gillen (1899: 122–5) and Roth (1903: 16–23) and resolutely rejected evidence which had a contrary implication, e.g. Purcell (1893: 286–9), Strehlow (1907: 2, 52, n. 7), Spencer & Gillen (1899: 265). Nearly all the more recent detailed ethnography leads to the conclusion that the formally expressed ignorance of physiological paternity is a kind of religious fiction – see in particular Warner (1937: 24), Thomson (1933: 506), Roheim (1932: 96–7), Sharp in Ashley-Montagu (1937: 163–3), Stanner (1933: 27–8), Meggitt (1962: 273). The case of Kaberry is discussed in greater detail below. Those who have maintained a version of the Hartland position down to recent times – and these include Malinowski, Ashley-Montagu, Stanner (1933) and Kaberry (1936, 1939) – have shown themselves willing to accept even the flimsiest evidence *for* the fact of ignorance, while evidence *against*, even when it is most meticulously recorded, is repeatedly rejected on the ground that it must be due to recent contaminating influence from mission stations or other Europeans. Thus Stanner (1933) reports of the Daly River Tribes that: 'It is clear that two theories of sex exist side by side: (*a*) a mystical theory of the type commonly found in Australian cultures and (*b*) a barely understood, confused version of the orthodox theory learnt from the whites.' Stanner has no evidence that (*b*) was in fact learnt from the whites. Thomson (1933) came down decisively on the other side: 'I actually approached the present study with a firmly rooted belief that the natives were entirely ignorant of the fact of physiological fatherhood. It was only after I was repeatedly made aware of the facts that I became convinced of the reality of the natives' knowledge.' Yet Kaberry (1936) could still persuade herself that ignorance of physiological paternity is a feature of ethnography reported from all over Australia without exceptions.

Meggitt's statements are discussed in my main text. Kaberry's two reports are especially interesting because they bear rather directly on Roth's original statement and because she herself quite uncritically accepts the view that the native beliefs and practices arose from 'ignorance of physical paternity'. Her fieldwork was carried out in the Kimberley Division of Western Australia about 800 miles due west of Roth's 'Tully River Blacks'. All her discussions with informants were conducted in pidgin English. Close attention to the details of her account do not support her theory that informants were ignorant of the physiology of sex in any simple sense. What they said, in quite explicit terms, is that they considered sexual intercourse a necessary but not sufficient cause of pregnancy. A woman does not become pregnant automatically as soon as she has sex relations; she becomes pregnant because she conceives and it is with the theology surrounding *conception* that Roth's account and also Kaberry's is largely concerned. Kaberry's version (1939: 42–3) clearly indicates the logic of Roth's story. The Kimberley natives said that spirit children were created long ago by the Rainbow Serpent and 'temporarily incarnated in animals, birds, fish, reptiles. Some say the spirit children are like children the size of a walnut; others that they resemble small red frogs. Conception occurs when one of these enters a woman. Its presence in the food given her by her husband makes her vomit, and later he dreams of it or else of some animal which he associates with it. It enters his wife by the foot and she becomes pregnant. The food which made her ill becomes the *djerin*, conception totem of her child.' In other words a woman recognizes that she is pregnant when she experiences 'morning sickness' – which is true also of European women.

'The husband of the woman is the social father of the child and as a rule its spiritual *genitor*, for it sometimes happens that the woman finds the *djerin* herself or that it is given to her by another man. The latter however will not dream of the spirit child, nor have access to the woman sexually nor exercise any rights over the child, who will take the country and the totems of the woman's husband. There were also instances where although the husband himself had found the *djerin* he did not afterwards dream of the child. But his wife would then assert that she had done so.' 'Questioned on the function of sexual intercourse natives admitted that it prepared the way for the entry of the spirit child. They asserted that a young girl could not bear children.' [Compare the similar materials in Malinowski (1913: 210–12).]

I am very puzzled as to how anyone could interpret such data as indicating 'ignorance of physical paternity'. Kaberry's informants are saying that conception is not predictable in advance but is recognized by certain physiological signs after the event. They say that sex relations are a necessary preliminary to this condition, and they say, as do most Europeans, that the foetal embryo has a soul. Their theological arguments are concerned with the origin of this soul. Since they are less attracted by the vitalistic fallacy than are orthodox Christians, they fail to make any precise distinction between the soul and the foetus. Instead of saying that the semen is a constituent of the foetus and that the soul is a metaphysical separate entity, they speak of the foetus-soul floating in semen 'like a water-lily'. Finally they assert that the woman's legally recognized sexual partner has an exclusive status as father of the child. This set of beliefs and attitudes seems to me to differ from that of the British only on rather subtle issues of a metaphysical kind, it certainly does not constitute physiological ignorance in any simple sense. That a distinguished anthropologist should once have thought otherwise displays the oddity of anthropologists rather than the oddity of the aborigines.

2 Spiro (1966: 112) maintains that the fact that a set of ritual data are structured in a manner which is directly parallel to a set of social relations is of no relevance unless we have direct evidence that the actors are consciously or unconsciously aware of the significance of this symbolism. Instead of looking for patterns in the way that people behave Spiro would adopt the naive procedure of asking the actor why he behaves as he does – 'and unlike some anthropologists, I believe him'. If Spiro tries this out in the case of English marriage procedures he will get some most astonishing results. These rituals are, as it happens, structured in an extremely clear and well-defined way, but not one bride in a thousand has even an inkling of the total pattern.

3 Frazer (1910: 1: 336) 'To a Central Australian father fatherhood means that a child is the offspring of a woman with whom he has the right to cohabit, whether he has actually had intercourse with her or not. To the European mind the tie between a father and his child is physical, to the Central Australian it is social.' Cf. Malinowski (1913: Ch. 6); Radcliffe-Brown (1931: 42); Ashley-Montagu (1937: Ch. 13).

4 Ishida (1964) reports on a wide range of oriental materials which were not available to Hartland.

5 Powell's report was as follows: '[I was told] the semen acts as a coagulant of the menstrual blood producing a "clot" which a spirit child (*baloma*) enters by way of the head or otherwise, and which proceeds to grow after the "quickening" by the entry of the *baloma*. My suggestions that this account either contradicted that of Malinowski or else was garbled "mission talk" were strenuously denied by my informants, who maintained that both accounts were "true", but that they were "different". Malinowski's, they said, was

"men's talk" valid in formal situations, e.g. in matters of land ownership and the like; the account given to me was "women's and children's talk", that is, it was what fathers or their sisters told children as they became old enough to take more than a childish sexual interest in the opposite sex.' (Powell 1956: 277–8. Quoted with author's permission.)

6 The evidence for 'dogma' is very clear. In 1909 the Bishop of North Queensland complained to Frazer that ignorance of the relation between intercourse and pregnancy 'forms a fact which has to be reckoned with in the introduction of a higher standard of morality among the aborigines, for they do not naturally accept the true explanation of conception and childbirth even after their admission to the mission stations' (Frazer 1909). In later references to the bishop's statement Frazer cites only the above remarks, but the aboriginal reluctance to accept the European viewpoint seems to have been a male peculiarity. The bishop also told Frazer: 'We often have girls who are sent to the mission *enceinte* and we never dwell on any wrongfulness of their condition. We have no trouble afterwards, neither have we found, at any rate for many years, that the girls persist in the belief … that copulation is not the cause of pregnancy'. Even more striking is Fortune's account (Fortune 1932: 239) of how he tried to stage a debate between Dobuans who maintained the role of the father and Trobrianders who denied it. 'But the head of every Dobuan in the room immediately was turned away from me towards the wall. They affected not to hear the conversation; but afterwards when they had me alone they were furious with me.' The argument was plainly about doctrine not about knowledge. Theologians who debate the doctrine of transubstantiation cannot usefully be accused of ignorance of the elementary facts of chemistry.

7 Two pages from the end of his three-volume work Hartland remarks: 'I cannot hide from myself the important bearing that some of the subjects dealt with in these pages may have upon Christian controversy'; but his heretical daring gets no further than that. Frazer is equally cautious. Frazer (1906: 349–50) draws attention to the writings of a variety of authors who have seen similarities between the Cult of Isis and the Cult of the Virgin Mary, but he scarcely comments on this point. Book 2, chapter 1 of this work, which is indexed 'Stories of Virgin Birth' never mentions Christianity at all.

8 All the numerous 'mother goddesses' of the Ancient

World seem to have been classified as 'virgins'. There may be complex problems of translation here. In the Trobriands, a widow, after the conclusion of her mourning, becomes a 'marriageable maiden' and is classified as such. It is at least possible that the title of 'virgin' accorded to such goddesses as Aphrodite signified their sexual availability rather than their physiological condition. Incidentally the original Hebrew of Isaiah vii. 14 which is quoted in Matthew i. 23 refers to a 'maiden' rather than to a 'virgin'.

# SELECTED BIBLIOGRAPHY

A list of the principal works of Edmund Leach,
with the dates of their first appearance

SOCIAL AND ECONOMIC ORGANIZATION OF THE ROWANDUZ
KURDS (London School of Economics Monographs
on Social Anthropology, no. 3, London, 1940)

SOCIAL SCIENCE RESEARCH IN SARAWAK (H.M.S.O. for
the Colonial Office, London, 1950)

POLITICAL SYSTEMS OF HIGHLAND BURMA (G. Bell & Sons
for the London School of Economics, London, 1954)

PUL ELIYA: A VILLAGE IN CEYLON (Cambridge University Press, Cambridge, 1961)

RETHINKING ANTHROPOLOGY (London School of Economics Monographs on Social Anthropology, no. 22,
The Athlone Press, London, 1961)

A RUNAWAY WORLD: THE REITH LECTURES, 1967 (The
British Broadcasting Corporation, London, 1968)

# THE AUTHOR

Edmund Leach, born in 1910, read Mathematics and Mechanical Sciences at Cambridge and obtained his B.A. in 1932. After several years of civilian life in China he returned to England and studied Social Anthropology under Malinowski and Raymond Firth. An abortive field trip to Kurdistan in 1938, frustrated by the Munich crisis, was followed by a prolonged trip to Burma in 1939, frustrated by the war. From autumn 1939 to the summer of 1945 he saw much of Northern Burma as an officer in the Burma Army. In 1947–8, he took his Ph.D., carried out a survey in Sarawak and took a first teaching appointment at L.S.E. He relinquished a Readership at this school in 1953 in order to return to Cambridge as Lecturer (1953–8), then Reader in Anthropology. In 1966, he succeeded Lord Annan as Provost of King's College, Cambridge. His 1967 Reith Lectures brought him to the attention of the general public but he continues his research work as one of this country's leading social anthropologists.